ATANDO CABOS

THEOLOGICAL EDUCATION BETWEEN THE TIMES

Ted A. Smith, series editor

Theological Education between the Times gathers diverse groups of people for critical, theological conversations about the meanings and purposes of theological education in a time of deep change. The project is funded by the Lilly Endowment Inc.

ATANDO CABOS

Latinx Contributions to Theological Education

Elizabeth Conde-Frazier

WILLIAM B. EERDMANS PUBLISHING COMPANY

GRAND RAPIDS, MICHIGAN

Wm. B. Eerdmans Publishing Co.
4035 Park East Court SE, Grand Rapids, Michigan 49546
www.eerdmans.com

Published 2021
Printed in the United States of America

27 26 25 24 23 22 21   1 2 3 4 5 6 7

ISBN 978-0-8028-7901-1

Library of Congress Cataloging-in-Publication Data

Names: Conde-Frazier, Elizabeth, author.
Title: Atando cabos : Latinx contributions to theological education /
    Elizabeth Conde-Frazier.
Description: Grand Rapids, Michigan : William B. Eerdmans Publish-
    ing Company, 2021. | Series: Theological education between the
    times | Includes bibliographical references. | Summary: "A histori-
    cal and sociological overview of Latinx Protestantism in the United
    States that reflects on how institutions of theological education
    might better welcome and incorporate the gifts of these popula-
    tions"—Provided by publisher.
Identifiers: LCCN 2021000750 | ISBN 9780802879011 (paperback)
Subjects: LCSH: Theology—Study and teaching—United States. |
    Hispanic American Protestants. | Protestantism—Social aspects—
    United States.
Classification: LCC BV4030 .C655 2021 | DDC 230.071/073—dc23
LC record available at https://lccn.loc.gov/2021000750

Contents

Acknowledgments

There is wisdom in the counsel of many (Prov. 15:22). How do you write in the midst of heavy administrative work, a change of employment, a cross-country move, and a dislocating house fire? Answer: With the loving support of a husband who is ever present and praying (love you, Ira) and a group of people whose insights, experience, encouragements, resources, and fellowship walked with me throughout a process of thinking, writing, and worshiping together, in the most creative ways. Thank you to Maria Liu Wong, Amos Yong, Keri Day, Hosffman Ospino, Chloe Sun, Mark Jordan, Willie James Jennings, Mark Young, Colleen Mary Mallon, OP, Daniel Aleshire, and Rachelle Green, who listened, inquired, and resourced my writing. Thanks to Ulrike Guthrie for editing with great sensitivity, for opening up the spaces of my thoughts, and thanks to Ted Smith for your affirmation, humility, and gracious leadership. Gracias Grace Vargas for assistance with historical research.

Agradecimiento especial to the teachers and nurturers of the soul of the Latin@ church (Sunday school teachers, Bible institute instructors and professors, denominational leaders, networkers, community organizers, and *comunidades de práctica*) for your witness of teaching with passion and faith. My greatest appreciation to the Asociación para la Educación Teológica Hispana (AETH) for opening a space for new creation and *teología en conjunto*, and to Fernando Cascante for giving me the luxury of time to write.

Introduction

My five-year-old granddaughter had just lost her first baby tooth. She was excited to hear that Ratoncito Perez (Mouse Perez) would be bringing a present in exchange for her tooth. In Latin American countries, he is the equivalent of the tooth fairy, a tradition that originated in Madrid in 1894. Cecilia wanted the gift but was reluctant to give up her tooth. Instead, she wanted to put it back so that her smile could stay the same. However, behind the fallen tooth the new tooth was already apparent, growing in and overlapping with where the old one had been. In theological education we are likewise in an overlapping time, a time when the passing season meets the coming one and the new season is still not entirely apparent. The old and the new intersect.

In this book I show how the two eras of theological education are already overlapping, interrelating, and coinciding. My hope is that by recognizing the similarities and common ground in the shapes of this theological education, we might better collaborate to implement a new educational design for the already arriving season.

When we are creating something in such a transitional, overlapping time, we are not always certain what materials and visions will fit best, and we may not have at hand what is needed. Such a time calls for experimentation. It is in this inventive interlude that we work at *atando cabos sueltos* (tying loose ends), ends for which we previously had no use because they seemed out of place and did not match the previous situation. For those

1

of us who have been poor, we understand that *cabos sueltos* are precisely the things that we do not discard because they are very helpful for inspiring us to think creatively. *Cabos sueltos* are still around when the last thing we made is already tattered and in disuse. But these materials are strong and have the right stuff for patching up and reinventing. Even while I speak of reinventing, in reality the understanding of Ecclesiastes holds true: "there is nothing new under the sun" (Eccles. 1:9).[1] But there is always perspective that comes from our present reflections on the past, combinations of things we haven't yet tried, and the fit of leftover ideas in different times and contexts.

My *cabos sueltos* are taken from a variety of sources. The first is the thread of my own theological education growing up in a Latin@[2] immigrant church in the city of New York. Theological education in the Latinx community is a continuum that goes from Christian education in a congregation to next-level study in a seminary. When I was fourteen, I taught fourth-grade Sunday school in this congregation. This meant that I was required to attend Bible study on Wednesday nights. After the study, Sunday school teachers would sit around the table with the pastor to discuss the theological points of the uniform lessons. The focus of the discussion was to consider the different theological points possible and to see where our preferences were. Mostly, the pastor wanted us to bring theological arguments that made sense and were biblically based. The pastor wanted to ensure that we were not pushing any particular point. While reminding us where our American Baptist denomination stood theologically, he wanted us to let persons choose where they stood as long as they could say why from a biblical standpoint. What I did not realize at the time was that the creation of a space for theological thinking with the capacity to hold on to a diversity of views was not the norm in many other contexts. These other contexts saw indoctrination as the purpose of biblical teaching.

Our pastor modeled this type of thinking and openness to differing views in his teaching and sermons as well, thus creating a consciousness of diversity and of the multiple ways to navigate theological and cultural diversity. This was a Latin@ church where the cultural diversity included many different Latin American countries, and sometimes Spain. Persons had come not only from different countries but also from different expressions of Christianity. Because our pastor always asked where a particular view came from, we learned to identify contexts with theological and historical differences. He would often fill in missing information. This was important for how we gave consideration to our layers of diversity.

A way to express our cultural diversity was on Pan-American Day, celebrated yearly on October 12.[3] At this celebration we wore our traditional dress and shared our histories, cultural traditions, foods, poetry, drama, music, and sometimes how we felt about having to immigrate, along with our hopes, dreams, and struggles. There were tears and many tastes at the table. We learned to say "*dime más*" ("tell me more") before making a judgment about each other's ways, which may have seemed strange at first encounter. These were diversity practices.

Our pastor held that to be Americanized was important if we were to progress while also understanding that bilingualism was a benefit. Our pastor was the Reverend Dr. Santiago Soto Fontánez, a Puerto Rican man who held a PhD from Columbia University in Spanish literature and had been a missionary and preacher to El Salvador. He was instrumental in establishing a school that is still operating in Santa Ana, sixty-four kilometers northwest of the capital city of San Salvador. Education was his forte. He was a tri-vocational pastor. While pastoring, he taught part time at Brooklyn College and also headed up what was then the Spanish Department of the American Baptist Churches of Metropolitan New York. This part of the work included church planting and ensuring that the new pastors were well prepared for the ministry. He became influential in the teaching that would continue to develop leaders for the continued "Spanish work." His work was so successful that from these congregations leaders were sent out to other parts of the United States to pastor and begin new congregations.

At Passover, Pastor Soto would bring a rabbi to explain the Passover. The rabbi pushed our usual understandings of "salvation." When he left, Pastor Soto would take our questions. He made it clear that it was fine not to have answers to the mystery of God's love for all the world. These theological discussions still form the grounding of my ecumenical and interfaith work.

Our congregation mentored its children, and so it was that my gifts for teaching and preaching were nurtured early. This meant that adults with similar gifts would come alongside the children to teach us, and we had opportunities to carry out ministry alongside our adult mentors. Children helped as ushers and visited and prayed for sick children in their homes (though not in hospitals, given the rules of these institutions). We served as deacons and helped to prepare communion. We helped in Sunday school and even in the kitchen, where both men and women cooked and served and had fellowship. Music, art, and drama were a part of our ministries as we shared the gospel in many ways, and we even put on comedies in the summer so as to bring joy. We learned to navigate our new environment by having bus trips in the summer. Neighborhood children were included in these, which meant that the church would sponsor them. Those families in the church who were better off would bring extra food for all. Their tables were open to everyone. Because their contributions included fresh produce I had never seen or tasted before—since, like most of us, my family was limited to buying food at the corner bodega—these meals felt like banquets.

The Hispanic churches of the American Baptist denomination had a Bible institute, and it entailed very serious study. Yearly we also held a variety of workshops in different churches for learning how to do ministry—as a deacon, usher, financial secretary, trustee, teacher, prison ministry worker, hospital visitor (today it would be like chaplaincy), minister with women, and other outreach ministry work. All this was part of my theological education before even attending seminary. In this context, theological education included Christian education. There was no real separation since everyone had a calling in the church to a particular ministry and was expected to prepare for that ministry. Such ministry included preaching, teaching, fellowship, and service to the community. All these varied opportunities are *cabos sueltos* that I have worked with as a theological educator.

Cabos sueltos arise in history. And so chapter 1 provides a brief history of Protestant missions and Christian education in Latin America and the Spanish-speaking Caribbean. This history depicts the roots of the structure of theological education today in the Latinx context. It presents the theological and structural foundations for the formats of theological education that have given shape to our present institutions. Two basic models of education are featured.

In chapter 2, I offer the theological *cabos sueltos* of the doctrines of the priesthood of all believers and of the *misión integral* (holistic mission) that together shape our understanding of church and its mission. These are the drivers of the purpose of theological education for the Latin@ church.

Chapter 3 discusses and illustrates curricular issues within the understanding of a contextual theology. It discusses and demonstrates epistemological and pedagogical matters for theological education for a globalized context.

Structure is a part of curriculum. Chapter 4 looks at interdisciplinary aspects, the diversity of theological thinking, and ecologies of education in the information age as a way of beginning to think about different perspectives and possibilities for the structure of theological education.

The fifth and final chapter of the book calls for a renewal of Reformation energies for the transformation of the church. It considers new, emerging, and surprising things to come, for *cabos sueltos* are sometimes new threads, assorted woods, buttons, beads, and other materials for which we need to find glues, shellacs, and paints that are not yet in our toolbox of supplies. We will need to search in new places and create fresh partnerships for learning to construct education with these newly discovered supplies.

Uncertainty, vulnerability, complexity, and ambiguity characterize our times and require urgent attention to creative collaboration. They call us to look beyond ourselves, to find those who think differently, whose life experiences and views bring perspectives we are not used to engaging for creating knowledge in community. For example, for the Association for Hispanic Theological Education (AETH), this diversity has come from our partnerships with the Association for Theological Schools (ATS); from the diversity of our members, who come from a variety of different regions in the United States; from Latin America; and from our first and second generation of Latinx peoples. They are on our board and on committees of our organization; they participate in monthly *conversatorios*, or conversations, on a variety of topics related to theological education; they participate in communities of practice that meet monthly so that the diversity of views regularly permeates the life of the organization.[4]

The Wabash Center for Teaching and Learning in Theology and Religion in 2020 offered a webinar on organizational change, collaboration, and creativity. Dr. Stephen Lewis and Dr. Matthew W. Williams identified and defined some of the competencies of institutional creativity.[5] Among these competencies are awareness of systems, observation of the underlying assumptions of the system and their basis, and organizational psychology, which helps us understand the behaviors that create our institutional culture and ways of communication. These competencies, among other things, teach us to read the financial picture with an understanding of how our cost systems and educational systems work in tandem.[6] My hope as you read this and the other books in the series is that you will seek to develop these competencies and to design creative collaborations across the board with your own *cabos sueltos*.

De Dónde Vienes y a Dónde Vas?

Roots of Latin@ Theological Education

On the main plaza of the University of Puerto Rico is a monument in honor of the Puerto Rican teacher. It features a man, a woman, and two children sharing a book. Close by is a bust of Eugenio Maria de Hostos, a master teacher and pedagogue famed throughout the Caribbean. These monuments speak to the importance of education and therefore to the way in which teachers are honored on the island. Education is not only about instruction or obtaining a degree. In Latina cultures, "an educated person" (*una persona educada*) is "a person who has a capacity for judgment, a training that allows him to know how to act in situations that arise. . . . A well-educated person must also have a set of ethical criteria and attitudes that make them apply them for justice and good work."[1] Teaching is more than a profession. It is a vocation and a very important part of the shaping of society, since it entails a calling to the art and science of forming persons with values that inform how they also carry out their purpose in the world such that they benefit and work toward the dignity of all created life. To be *una persona educada* is to treat others in a way that they can tell we are educated by our refined and humble bearing.

Whenever a new church, or a group that seeks to respond to a spiritual hunger in a particular area, is about to start, it begins with a Bible study or with a vacation Bible school for children rather than with a space for worship. The same holds true for laypersons or pastors who come to the United States from Puerto Rico. Why is this? The missionaries who first came to Puerto Rico started their work in the same manner. The first persons who connected the missionaries to the "pueblo" to which they came were teachers, and the first pastors were teachers. How did this come about?

The purpose of this chapter is to present the origins of theological education in the Latin@ community by tracing the historical roots of the missionary work and the political, economic, and theological context from the end of the nineteenth century to the end of the twentieth century. It presents only a general overview of some of the defining movements and theologies that influenced the beginnings of the Protestant church and theological education, which in turn have shaped what theological education is for the Latin@ church today. The complexity of these movements and theologies continues to create differences among us and oppression that keeps us from defining a theological education that could be more relevant for our contexts. It also offers the blessing of a strong foundation for equipping persons in traditional ministry. As you read, you may want to ask yourself how this legacy influences your thinking and how it might limit the ways that theological education may need to respond to the equipping of the many who are called into a diversity of ministries for our times.

The Political, Economic, and Theological Context of Missionary Work

Protestantism came to Latin America and to the Caribbean as part of a colonizing agenda as much as an evangelizing one. The creation of institutions to embed the Protestant expression of Christianity also had this dual purpose. Along with the church, one of the most important institutions is education in its different forms and levels: primary, secondary, vocational, university, and theological. To understand how these educational institutions develop, one needs at least a basic understanding of the political and economic framework in which events of the missionary endeavor from the United States to Latin America took place. In the documents of the nineteenth and early twentieth century, the United States is referred to as North America. Therefore, throughout this chapter, I use this term too.

From the mid-1800s to the early 1900s, the United States expanded its economic interests abroad, as industry and commerce needed places for both production and consumption. The United States robbed or usurped the resources of other countries for its own production and merchandising. To defend its interests in these countries, the United States used a variety of policies such as the Monroe Doctrine, in which President James Monroe declared "America for the Americans" as a protection against the risk that the consolidated European countries of the 1814 restoration would seek to gain position in Latin America. This secured Latin America as a zone of political control and commercial hegemony for the United States.[2] The Monroe Doctrine was later amended by Theodore Roosevelt's promise to wield a "big stick" in the Roosevelt Corollary of 1904. It called for the United States to "police" the Caribbean and Latin American countries by helping them to "do away with political instability and financial mismanagement that could invite European intervention that could undermine the independence of the republics within the hemisphere."[3] To implement this policy, the United States claimed the right to intervene with military force in any dispute between Latin American countries or against other world powers active in these countries, with the ostensible purpose of restoring order. This the local countries saw as high-handed, as it interfered with their self-determination. President Theodore Roosevelt rationalized his actions on the basis of Manifest Destiny, a philosophy with theological underpinnings that gave to the United States a civilizing role, allowing it to "coerce a nation which by selfish action stood in the way of measures that could benefit the world as a whole."[4]

In this political climate, missionaries from North America and some European countries, as well as some Latin American delegates, came together in 1916 to discuss the missionary project in Latin America. This gathering was called the Panama Congress. The participants rejected armed intervention and the economic interests behind it. Latin American participants did not fail to mention during their discussions the "violent materialism and greed" of the Pan-American Railroad, one of the large companies expanding on the continent.[5]

The missionaries took a stance against armed interventionism in Latin America. Among them, individuals such as Guy Inman and Stanley Rycroft promoted a different Pan-Americanism, one that places itself at the service of a growing relationship between the United States and Latin America and addresses economic, socioeconomic, and educational matters between them.[6] From a theological standpoint, while the missionaries denounced the corruption and injustices of the companies that exploited resources in Latin America, they did not critique the political structure of Pan-Americanism that opened the door to these injustices. The missionaries saw the oppressive policies only as a result of the individual moral defects of a few individuals.[7]

In the United States, different thinkers presented two democratic models. One, represented by C. B. Macpherson, was democracy as protection; the other was democracy as development. The first accepts a capitalist society ruled by the market. Undergirding it is the utilitarian philosophy of Jeremy Bentham, which seeks to maximize collective happiness. In practice, the most common quantitative measure for happiness was *money.* In this understanding, money is the instrument with which one measures pain or pleasure, and the function of the government is to protect the interests of capitalist society and present those interests as inherently fair (even when they are not).

Democracy as development emerged as a response to the toll that the greed of industrialization had taken on the working class. John Stuart Mill and John Dewey, among others, did not accept that industrial progress would automatically help workers in their struggle to "make it." Instead, they proposed democracy as development, a view that sees each person as trying to "achieve betterment as a moral being . . . who seeks development."[8] Advancing toward this goal requires a greater distribution of resources to the poor and the working class. How this is done becomes the contentious point. For some of these thinkers, such as Mill, the vote is a way to secure equity. For Robert McIver, the way is for the people, not the state, to play a greater role in creating cooperatives and to engage in creating more representative political parties. Finally, for Dewey, "education is the way."[9] Dewey saw democracy as an ethical idea more than as a political system. As such, knowledge, skills, and character were to be nurtured by teachers.[10] Dewey contributed the objective of "developing a better generation." Míguez Bonino posits that Dewey's is "the idea that predominates in Panama 1916."[11] He claims that for the liberal Protestant missionary agenda, this concept of development brings together the social, religious, and political strands. The interpretation of the telos of this democratic vision is married to a liberal theology that integrates ethical concerns and personal development so that the motto for education becomes "education that builds character."[12]

Therefore, those who met in New York to plan the Congress of Panama tasked one of their eight work commissions with a focus on education. The education commission provided important information about the different countries, in particular Chile. When the Panama Congress finally took place in 1916, its participants included teachers from educational institutions.

The documents of the Edinburgh conference in 1913 served as a model for the Panama Congress. They addressed the role of education in the evangelizing mission and suggested that education was important not only for socioeconomic reasons but also for discipleship. They proposed that attention be paid to the condition of the poor and especially of orphans, since education is the vehicle to train them for a better life, inculcate values, and keep them from the temptations that trap the poor and threaten their survival.[13]

A few dominant theological viewpoints influenced the missionaries. One was the Social Gospel, whose leading proponents included Walter Rauschenbusch, Washington Gladden, Lyman

Abbott, and Charles Loring Brace. They sought to arouse the consciences of their parishioners and of society regarding the social concerns of an industrialized society. They addressed and advocated for issues such as ensuring workers' rights to form unions, preventing child labor, earning a living wage, regulating factories, and providing housing for working people. Through their writing, preaching, and social activism—as in the case of Brace, who founded the Children's Aid Society of New York City— they promulgated Social Gospel teachings and practices. In the missionary field in Latin America, one of the more prominent leaders was Samuel Guy Inman who expressed the Social Gospel through an educational agenda. His work is featured below.

Latin American theologians today critique the Social Gospel, and democracy as development, as incompatible with the expressions of the US version of Pan-Americanism in Latin America. Moreover, for the most part, these ideals did not find traction beyond the small church communities of liberal Protestants. Because they did not penetrate into the fundamentalist and Holiness churches, they ran counter to other missionary expressions brought to Latin America.[14]

During the 1840s, evangelical missionaries—who were mostly Presbyterians, Methodists, and Baptists—came to Latin America. Among the main points of their theology was absolute belief in the Bible as the Word of God, as "God-breathed [given by divine inspiration] and ... profitable for instruction, for conviction [of sin], for correction [of error and restoration to obedience], for training in righteousness [learning to live in conformity to God's will, both publicly and privately—behaving honorably with personal integrity and moral courage]."[15] These evangelicals prioritized sharing the message of salvation of sinners through the death of Jesus on the cross, and were completely persuaded that acceptance of this message could change a person into a moral and virtuous individual capable of doing the will of God on earth and having eternal life with God after death. This theology and its proponents had emerged from the Second Great Awakening crusades of Charles Finney, Timothy Dwight, and others. These took place in burgeoning urban areas, in colleges and universities, and among the middle class. At first, the religious experience of conversion was connected with social reform, and therefore the evangelists of the awakening took on moral issues of their day such as slavery and poverty. Because religious awakening, social progress, and education were interwoven, these evangelicals believed they could create a society that could mirror the kingdom of God and would then inspire other nations in this direction. Evangelical missionaries brought this tradition to Latin America and the Caribbean.

Theological Positions among Missionaries in Latin America

This is not the place to discuss thoroughly the theological positions of the different missionary groups. Instead, I briefly present the positions that most influenced the Latin American church, and do so even to this day, and I discuss the ways in which these positions fashioned Christian education and the types of institutions that transmit the faith and prepare leadership for the church. In particular, I look at the beginnings of how fundamentalist and Pentecostal traditions shaped Protestant faith in Latin America.

In José Míguez Bonino's analysis of the different theological forces that forged Protestantism in Latin America, he claims that "the development of evangelical piety is the real substratum of Latin American missionary Protestantism."[16] Therefore, the different theological camps come from movements influenced by the second awakening. Míguez Bonino agrees with Pablo Deiros and others that the three main strands of theological thought were liberationists, conservatives, and fundamentalists.[17] Around 1916, evangelicalism was marked by individualism, a more subjective soteriology, and emphasis on sanctification. While these missionaries held liberal political viewpoints, the practice of faith and piety did not sustain or give full expression to these understandings.[18] After 1930, the Protestantism that the Protestant missionary promulgated was represented by the

Holiness movement as well as the millennial and fundamentalist streams. After World War II, the missionaries that had been forced to return to the United States from China, India, and Eastern European countries went to Latin America.[19] This new wave of missionaries gave greater expression to an "otherworldly theology" that was influenced mainly by premillennial fundamentalism. It described a dualism between the world and the spirituality that Christians were to have. Practices included a series of legalisms and withdrawal from the world. Míguez Bonino observes that these practices cause significant doctrinal distortion, and that this paralyzes the people, keeping them from places of liberation while also dividing them from one another. The Social Gospel influence was also present among the earlier group of missionaries, and later we will see their influence in an educational agenda that included the different arenas of persons' lives, including the political and economic.

As these different influences took hold in Latin America, the liberal understanding forged a Latin American Protestant worldview in which, by way of conversion, one could re-create one's identity and have a self-consciousness that promoted becoming assertive and taking initiative (by making a decision for Christ beyond the cultural and family ties). This prepared one to participate in a more democratic and modern life. The *iglesias históricas* (mainline churches) became known for having an ethos of "bourgeois liberalism," since the experience of conversion was connected to aspirations of upward mobility. They also had a sense of religious freedom and associated the way of the kingdom with human progress as seen in North America. Protestantism, therefore, leaned politically toward the parties that would grant it religious freedom. At that time in Latin America, these tended to be parties on the left.

After the 1940s, a tension arose among the churches. The premillennial missionaries had greater influence, and the tension between their advocacy of social action and the priority of evangelization was transmitted to Latin America. At the Latin American Protestant Conference (CELA I) in Buenos Aires, the

International Evangelical Council entered the proceedings and denounced liberal and communist modernism. This forced existing organizations to take a side. As a result, some of the existing Protestant organizations ruptured into two camps: those maintaining active social witness and ecumenism, whose theology emphasized God's work in history, and those who identified with separatist fundamentalism.[20]

The liberal and the conservative theologies and the expressions of the missionary work that emerged from them were in tension with one another. The approach and the telos of mission were different for each, and therefore influenced the teachings of the missionaries as they shared the gospel. The curriculum of the educational institutions, the outreach and levels of conversations with other entities and persons of power in society, took shape according to the focus and scope of the theology of the missionary.

Since the liberal proponents of the Social Gospel viewed education as a way of bettering society, they sought to have conversations with the intellectual classes and promoted political debates. They also promoted education that included more than teaching the Bible, such as classes in literacy, agriculture, and dance. The conservative group viewed education as a means to bring people to personal salvation and discipleship. Rooting the gospel in a particular country or culture was the goal of both of these groups, but the dimensions of life that they believed were to be engaged by the gospel determined what aspects of life their educational models engaged.

Educational Ideas

In North America, ideas of democracy and particularly of the extension of voting were gaining traction at the end of the nineteenth and the beginning of the twentieth century as society shifted from agrarianism to industrialization. The common good and ethical social concerns were important during this shift. Dewey believed that hopes, expectations, standards, and opinions were transmitted by communication of habits of doing, thinking, and feeling from the older generation to the younger.[21] These dimensions of learning and developing became a part of the religious education association and were the focus of much writing during the twentieth century and through the beginning of the twenty-first century.

Dewey focused mainly on the development of persons, and therefore the advancement of community. Important to him were cooperation and a greater distribution of goods and political representation. He understood education as a way to develop a better generation. The teacher was to nurture knowledge, skills, and character. The way to do this was defined as follows: "to put prayer daily in the mouths of those who are not Christians. Religious teaching in schools and colleges must be the same for Christians and non-Christians. Education is to train in the practices of devotional life creating the importance of very large habits. Habits of private and public prayer, of devotional use of the Bible and of the practice of the presence of God."[22]

To this end, missionaries worked with the teachers of the towns in Asian countries. The supervision of the primary missionary schools was carried out by the missionaries. The training of native teachers was considered work of a specialized nature, for the teachers had to be trained at a high level. Their training emphasized efficiency in all missionary educational work. Native teachers were going to be part of this commission of Christian education.[23] This echoed what those missionaries had learned in Asia, where a teacher was considered a "man of influence and an educated man." As such, they reported, "his opinions are sought on issues relating to life and, especially, in matters of religion on the part of the villagers. The entire area may change as a result of the opening of a school in the village under a fully Christian teacher."[24]

For them, the goal of education was the formation of character that influenced values and decision making as well as daily habits. Over the course of time, the purpose of education was to leaven persons' characters with Christian thinking and to guide them in daily life with noble and Christian ideals that they would promulgate in the new society with which they were interacting. Christian schools were meant to develop the new leaders of a society.[25]

These sentiments and strategies were what missionaries took with them to the Panama Congress in 1916. Reflected in them is the understanding that to Christianize a group or a nation was to change entirely the existing ideologies, replacing them with a Christian worldview. A worldview is the predominant set of opinions and beliefs about the world that drives a person, time, or culture, and it is the place from which all that exists is interpreted.[26] It is a set of beliefs that allows us to analyze and recognize reality from our own existence. Religions, philosophical systems, and political doctrines form such worldviews, since they provide a framework by which to interpret reality and to develop certain ethical and moral standards.[27]

Ideologies are part of the ingredients of a worldview. An ideology is primarily the widely shared beliefs, attitudes, and behaviors that are incorporated into social practices and institutional life. An ideology creates a logic that allows it to stand in the midst of other ideologies as well as to adapt to social changes. Generating a new ideology and conscience implies the creation of experiences of sufficient depth, duration, and intensity to permit the lenses of predominant interpretations to be transformed. When that is done, we increase the possibility of evangelization and Americanization.

Discipleship is the dimension of evangelization that works to shape in a person the values of the kingdom of God. Every ideology has an ethic that gives shape to principles and practices of morality. Christian educator Roberto Pazmiño explains that "Christian ethics deals with the reality of sin and the Christian call to service and sacrifice in the world."[28] For the Christian, values embody theological considerations and are concerned with what is virtuous, significant, and lasting. From these emanate the goals, ideals, and patterns of the limits of human thought and behavior for everyday life.[29]

These values are then the basis for judging all forms of human behavior and the different ideologies that support other forms and systems of living. For example, what is it to be children of God? This question leads us to the spiritual value of the salvation of people from their sin so that they may be free from sin and live just lives before God as God's adopted creatures by the power of Jesus's sacrifice and his redemptive blood. The Holy Spirit helps us to live according to the values of the kingdom: faith, justice, and love, among others. To walk in the Spirit is to live according to the Word of God with a feeling of adoration and admiration for the abundant life that Christ gives us.

Discipleship teaches us the way of thinking, or the arguments we use to understand life according to the will of God, as well as the acceptable practices of children of God based on the Word of God. The congregation, and its system of interpreting and teaching the Word of God, is a formational community through its teaching of the Word of God. It is also a community that keeps its members accountable to living in accordance with the teaching as a way of supporting its members in these practices and reinforcing the ways of thinking. On the basis of the values of the gospel, we verify which thoughts are considered faithful to the gospel and which are not. We suggest instead alternatives that are coherent with biblical values. The values are the different educational forms that ensure this and that seal the gospel as a new worldview.

Christian education aims to develop in persons the ability and willingness to participate and respond to the spiritual and social results of the gospel in order to remain in the divine work in the world. It seeks to nurture the development of a Christian worldview that is contextualized in the life of each person.[30] Education shapes society. The institutions of society, such as the family, the church, the community, the economy and its agencies (banks, real estate), the legal system (the courts), health-care institutions (hospitals, clinics), and the mass media (newspapers, radio, TV, the Internet), serve as the axes of education. These form different combinations called configurations that reinforce each other toward a common goal as part of the dissemination of the ideology one wants to establish. Throughout its history, the church has developed agencies and instruments through which it has fulfilled its teaching task in relation to the other axes or institutions of society. This is why evangelization and Americanization, Christian theology, and the values of the economic and political system are so closely interwoven.

It is through these means and educational configurations that the gospel message is transmitted to succeeding generations. In so doing, they certify, preserve, transmit, and transform the values and perspectives of the life of the community in general. To carry this out, these missionaries employed various means of education: Sunday schools, textbooks, creeds, commentaries, sermons, catechisms, spiritual disciplines, church services, seminaries and biblical institutes, and Christian colleges and universities. Pazmiño observes that "Christian movements have had an impact in terms of defining realities, evaluating and rationally interpreting behavior and the development of social visions."[31]

In analyzing the Protestant schools in Guatemala as part of the mission of evangelization of liberal Protestantism, Carlos Raúl Sosa Saliézar, program coordinator of the licentiate in theology at SETECA (Central American Theological Seminary) and member of the Lutheran church, discusses the emphasis on dialogue as part of the four dimensions of the missiology of liberal Protestantism during the first part of the twentieth century: "Protestants understand the mission as an intelligent dialogue with other sectors whose intellectual honesty was respectable."[32] To do this, they focused on the Latin American elite and the missionaries. They engaged in a dialogue with Latin American culture and thought. Examples of such missionaries were John Mackay and Alberto Rembao, who sought to make correlations between Latin American culture and the gospel. Rembao proposed an evangelical culture for Latin America.[33] In his book *The Conquest of America*, Jorge P. Howard says that an important aspect of his ministry was the conferences in schools and university centers, particularly the discussion period at the end of those

CHAPTER 1

conferences, which elicited a flood of questions. Among those attending the conferences were communists, socialists, theosophists, and university students.[34]

The missionary movements established missionary schools and, in some cases—as in Puerto Rico—they did it before the governments of the countries established a public education system. In both cases, the missionary schools exercised much influence in the broader society and established pedagogical and even religious principles as part of education. For example, John Mackay arrived in Peru as director of the Anglo-Peruvian School, one of the many American schools in Peru, Colombia, and Venezuela that are still very influential to this day. Schools were very important in the development of Protestantism. In Brazil, thirteen educational institutions were established by Presbyterian missionaries between 1870 and 1930, and used North American pedagogical methods.[35] These institutions catalyzed educational reform in Brazil.

Models of Education

To illustrate the ways that education, through Protestantism, was implemented in Latin America, I analyze two different models of education, one in Mexico and one in Puerto Rico. The Mexican model gives expression to the theology of the social gospel, while the educational work in Puerto Rico exemplifies a conservative theology at work.

In Mexico, the Protestant efforts were greatly influenced by Samuel Guy Inman. In his letters he maintained that preaching was an inadequate way of teaching the ways of religion. He placed the emphasis of his work on loving the people rather than building the institution. This was one of the criticisms that he directed toward the Roman Catholic Church in Latin America. He made a distinction between a living word and words about theories. For that reason, he moved from his missionary quarters to an apartment in downtown Monterrey, where he was more visible to the people, and the people to him. He then turned his home into a social center and gave everyone access to his personal library. Place is an important epistemological aspect. The knowledges that would interact with one another in this new space, and the relationship they would have to one another, would become important to the power and message of the gospel in Mexico.[36]

Inman was sent to Mexico to evangelize. While living with the people and sinking into the reality that Protestantism in Mexico was not advancing, he decided on a different method—that of carrying the social gospel to Mexico. He began doing this by "opening up a reading room, teaching English and forming a debate club to discuss problems of social ills and moral questions."[37]

In 1908, he and his wife were transferred to the frontier district, to a city named Ciudad P. Diaz, a mining town opposite Eagle Pass, Texas. They were the only missionaries in the area. It was there that he started the Instituto del Pueblo (The People's Institute). The Institute taught night classes in English and offered music lessons. Inman wanted it to become a social and intellectual center that would lead to the "betterment" of the Mexican people. This goal led him away from the usual missionary educational models. Inman had a gift for building relationships with persons of influence in the community: professionals, businesspersons, and those involved in governing. This educational strategy and community building prospered the work on the frontier. A year later, he raised funds to buy a building and thus expand the work of the Instituto. The new building had two floors and served as his family's living quarters, the center, and a public guest room for "distinguished official visitors to the city."[38] In this way, he continued to meet and influence many notable people, including the governor of Coahuila, Mr. Venustiano Carranza, who later became president of Mexico.

The new center tended to many different aspects of people's lives and therefore offered night classes, a free clinic, games, a debate club, a humane society, and Bible study. The center had a reading room; a circulating library; lectures and motion pictures on hygiene, agriculture, political science, and life problems; as well as a Victrola for playing music.

A sign of how the people and their governor valued the center was that the local government contributed one hundred dollars a month to its night-school program. While the Christian Women's Board of Missions recognized the importance and contributions of the center, in their letters they also pressed Inman to give greater emphasis to Christianizing the people.[39] Inman, however, believed that the Christian education work often duplicated the educational work of the states and their schools, while the Instituto, he claimed, provided something that no one else was doing.

The work at the center continued throughout the years of the Mexican Revolution, and the Instituto became a center for political life. Inman understood the civil war to be a result of the economic and sociopolitical oppression of the poor, including the indigenous population, by the land barons and the priests. For this reason he insisted that the people change their morals rather than their creed. Kenneth Woods writes that the People's Institute became the place for the discussion of social and political issues that could not be discussed elsewhere.[40] The Instituto also gave physical and mental aid to the people during this challenging time.

Inman's vision and philosophy were to provide for the interests and needs of the people so as to bring life in a holistic way. To this end, he gave aid to the forces of the Constitutionalists, who fought against the dictator's forces. The Constitutionalists were led by his friend Carranza. Carranza's forces captured the city of Piedras Negras, where the Instituto was located (the name of the city had changed), and they set up their headquarters across the street from the center. Because the soldiers used the maps, books, and typewriters of the center, it is little wonder that the center's students joined the rebel army. Many of the students later became governing leaders and public school superintendents in different states across Mexico. In the meantime, as the revolution dragged on, most other mission work closed.

The Instituto del Pueblo viewed education as a process for discussions and the sharing of knowledge that would integrate the various aspects of life. It provided for the people's needs during a vulnerable time of transition in their history. The success of the work depended on a great deal of tact, diplomacy, and nerve. Its foundation was the theology of the Social Gospel.

When Inman left to work on the Protestant Ecumenical Committee on Cooperation in Latin America in 1915, the work was turned over to a missionary who followed the general missionary movement and "pressured the students into reading the Bible and forced the Anglo-Saxon Christ upon them."[41] Inman's work had gained the support of the members of the upper class by operating from a gospel that addressed the social concerns of the people. In his continued work in Latin America, he lectured in the universities of Latin America, as did other missionaries with similar theological (and political) underpinnings.

In 1913, Inman established a second institute, in San Antonio, Texas, called the Mexican Christian Institute. It was a community house that offered classes; it also provided recreational facilities, a clinic, a library, and a counseling center. In 1961, to honor its founder, it became the Inman Christian Center. Today it serves the needs of low-income families in the inner city of San Antonio.

A different theological influence can be seen in Puerto Rico, where the educational work was pervaded by conservative theology. The focus of education was on the explicit teaching of the Bible and the individual salvation of persons. The schools established by the missionaries in rented houses or school buildings built by some denominations had "North American teachers and principals with some Puerto Rican assistants for the strict supervision of the missions and the sponsorship of women's missionary societies in the United States."[42] The curriculum included the study of the Bible and sometimes required students to attend Sunday school.

The Panama Conference report identified the objectives of the missionary schools in the following way: "The formation of children and young people under the influence of Christianity and its principles of conduct . . . the permeating of all society with Christian principles and ideals in all aspects of life. . . . Education fulfills its objective, without creating better ideals and moral conditions of effective life in society."[43] Therefore, much emphasis and support were placed on all levels of education, from kindergartens to universities and vocational schools. This was because Catholics attacked public education for the same reasons that Protestants defended it and saw it as a vehicle to form "reliable leaders in all vocations[,] especially to supply leaders for missionary work in Latin America."[44] This included the education of women.

One dimension of great influence in achieving change in the culture and worldview of the people was the Bible school or Sunday school. This simple method of studying the Bible by interpreting the text and applying it to the daily life of the people had a real effect on poor communities that were deprived of educational, cultural, and recreational resources. The media had been used to promote these studies. "Sunday school is an experience of . . . cultural education, of religious reflection on personal development and is carried out in a group with the objective that its members reflect on their life and the possibilities of change."[45] These started in 1905, and decades later comments still abound on the influence of biblical schools and how they trained thousands of young people who now occupy important positions in public schools, in commerce, and in other important areas of society. The Sunday school, together with the preaching, exercised great influence on the conscience of the people.[46] The teachings were forming people's habits of daily life, such as devotional life and daily prayer in public places.

Also formational were the *sociedades* (societies) of children, young people, men, and women. These *sociedades* helped to create a new mentality and expand social roles among Protestants in everyday life. The organizations, which were guided by their own elected officers, offered programs and discussion groups, shaped budgets, planned assemblies, and implemented parliamentary laws that produced a new form of socialization and new social actors. These groups facilitated the creation of new support networks for the new faith family that was born and was living in a countercultural way to the broader Hispanic-Catholic culture. In some cases, the active participation of women in these societies and the insistence that women study were creating a new awareness and sense of agency in women.

While the North American missionaries did exert control over the ecclesial institutions, at the same time it was their intent to maintain a balance between control and democracy with the purpose of promoting the marked difference between the Hispanic-Catholic culture and the American Protestant culture. In truth, though this was their intention, the missionaries who held to the tenets of the theology of the Social Gospel did not always implement such shared leadership.

Ecumenical Efforts

To carry out these efforts to change a society, the union of churches was important. This was done by appealing to the people's patriotic feeling while minimizing any anti-American spirit.[47] This aligns the ecumenical strategy with the educational strategy. Thus, institutions for theological education were founded, such as the Evangelical Seminary of Puerto Rico (1919), formed by the Disciples of Christ, Methodists, United Brethren and Presbyterians; the Evangelical Seminary of Theology in Matanza, Cuba (1946), formed by the Methodists, Presbyterians, and Episcopalians; and the Higher Institute of Theological Studies in Buenos Aires (1884), formed by the Waldensians, Methodists, and Disciples of Christ, and then joined by the Presbyterians and Lutherans.[48] Today, the ecumenical collaboration continues, and the emphasis is on expanding the theological education agenda to face the effects of globalization and to develop practical and contextual theology by doing theology from and within the Latin American context and culture using means of continuing education such as extensions and online programs.

Different theological lines existed in the formation of all these forms and educational agencies. One such was the fundamentalists, who did not see the importance of establishing social institutions to educate, heal the body, and regenerate the societies, since they focused on change at the individual level and thought that it was necessary to separate from the world in order to be ready for the second coming of Christ. Evangelization was a project of preaching to create changes in everyday life for the beginnings of faith in a countercultural way, creating a rupture with the past. It was a construction of new social and cultural practices.

Others held that Christ would not come until he was preached to every creature. They believed that it was necessary as part of perfecting society to use the scientific method to solve poverty. They saw the political regime as part of the regeneration of the world. For these believers, the missionary project was a civilizing project, and educational, medical, theological, journalistic, and other institutions were established to give form and strength to a Protestant foundation within the society, creating an American concept of the world. The ecumenical and theological expressions sought to focus on national and spiritual or otherworldly goals, thus hiding the colonialism and Americanizing agenda that each theological vision created out of what was originally an evangelizing missionary faith. Well-intentioned missionaries sought to hide this not only from the people but also from themselves.

A Latin American Church and Identity

In 1962, the International Office of Social Research of FERES published a volume on Protestantism in Latin America, authored by Prudencio Damboriena, SJ.[49] In the third chapter, on pastoral formation, Damboriena begins by recognizing two important factors: First, the rooting of the church in missionary territory depends on the balance between the solidarity and identification of the clergy with the people. Second is the element of estrangement between the foreign missionaries and the people of Latin America due to their different cultural roots. He explains that the cultural shock that comes as a product of evangelization and the effectiveness of the religious penetration is inversely proportional to the degree and amount of foreign culture that accompany that religious element. The balancing element of that equation is the native clergy who may be a part of that religious element because they are a part of the culture. This cultural knowledge is what makes possible the religious dialogue of the native clergy with their own people.

This insight is an epistemological key to the grounding of the gospel in the Americas. Those already located in the culture have knowledge of the culture, and this facilitates a deep dialogue about religious matters that is essential for rooting the gospel in a new location.[50] In contrast, the knowledge of the US culture with which missionaries came and which was their tool for explaining and imagining the gospel in the countries where they were, created a parallel life to that of the people's, and it necessitated that converts live a countercultural life.

The new life they lived was a pious and devoted life, one of living in the world but not being of the world. When dealing with political questions from within this framework, the church learned to be apolitical because such matters were "of the world." The other option was to separate one's political activity from one's religious activity. As such, the gospel did not leaven that arena of life and did not gain a place in the theological or diaconal expressions of the church. Social justice was not a part of the understanding of the kingdom of God. Jesus's kingdom was not of this world.[51]

This apolitical expression left new converts open to the Americanizing that took place as part of evangelization, and open to the missionaries who, unbeknownst to themselves, were the Americanizers who were in relationship with the people. This relationship made it more difficult for the people to separate the message from the messenger and to do a critique of the gospel "à la US" in order to understand the gospel for their own culture. This continues to be a tension, as the autochthonous leaders take the helm of the work. Theological education is a place where this tension can be felt.

Damboriena's report names this tension. It argues that from the beginning, even from the Panama Congress, the official min-

CHAPTER 1

utes of meetings did not reflect a forward-looking agenda that
included the formation of indigenous pastors. He points out that
this was due to a lack of trust in the peoples of South America
(this term was used to refer to all countries south of the United
States), given their small numbers, to take on such a responsibility. Furthermore, the accompanying politics of the United States
toward its southern neighbors did not inspire the sentiment of
Christian community but seemed to be guided instead by im-
positions. The foreign missionaries were reprimanded for not
including the nationals in the administrative duties, but actions
were not taken nor was there any system of accountability set
up to rectify the matter.[52] To help counteract this spirit of impo-
sition, missionaries saw the preparation of a national body of
pastors as necessary for the "conversion of the intellectual class
of citizens in the different countries."

The recruitment and formation of persons for ministry took
different shapes. One was doing more work among college students. Another was sending students to the United States to
study. The formation of pastors in their own countries entailed
a process of shadowing an already busy pastor for a brief time.

Centros *and* Seminarios

Besides such formation, *centros* (centers) named *seminarios* (sem-
inars) were established for more systematic instruction. In Mexico
there were two *centros*. One was run collaboratively by the Methodists and Presbyterians, the other by the Baptists. There were also a
few Bible institutes, which tended to be less systematic and were
for laypersons as well as lay pastors. At Santiago de Chile, the Methodists and the Presbyterians had another small seminary, as well
as one in Puerto Rico, one in Buenos Aires, and two in Brazil. While
the missionaries reported other such *centros*, in reality the students
studied part time and the curriculum included only a few courses
that were essential for the pastorate. The spaces where the *centros*
were located were not always conducive to study; the number of
candidates was in the single digits, and at times there was only one
professor who taught all the courses.[53]

28

By the time of the Protestant Congress of 1925 in Montevideo, the progress of the missionary work could be felt, as could the greater world power of the North Americans. A collection of the complaints of the Latin American delegates around the discriminatory treatment of the native pastors found a listening ear in Brewster Browning, a native evangelist. He stated that the North Americans had not shown the capacity to free themselves from their superiority complex. He accused the missionaries of saving for themselves the more fruitful places of ministry along with the better pay these offered, thus compromising the native pastors' innate capacity to be effective in the work.[54]

At the 1929 conference in Havana, Cuba, the issues of pastoral formation centered on the question of united seminaries and the importance of giving priority to national problems in the curriculum, including courses on the history of Spain and Latin America as well as literature, philosophy, sociology, economics, and politics of the people rather than the politics and disciplines pertaining to the United States. The list of priorities included an insistent recommendation to the North American missionaries that they get to know the peoples of South America better, specifically their language and customs.

An extensive report offered by Yorke Allen Jr., in a volume published by Harper and Brothers of New York, includes a long list of schools divided into different categories.[55] At the top were theological colleges, for students who had a bachelor's degree and could be taught in English (if they were not sent to the United States). Theological studies at the theological colleges were for three years, and students received a bachelor of divinity upon completion. The next tier of schools was theological schools, for which students needed to have received a high school diploma, or to have completed middle school if they studied at a US school. They also studied for three years and they received an L.TH. (*licenciado en teología*) or a B.TH. (*diplomado de bachiller en teología*). These were not accredited degrees but were conferred by the missionary societies.[56] Major cities in Latin America where churches had been started had a seminary. The number of students at these institutions could range from two to sixty, and the number of professors, from one to twelve. Seminaries were usually collaborative efforts.[57]

Theological education in the Latin@ context comes from this history with its wide range of efforts, including evangelism for a faith that too often took the North as normative, discipleship that created a new worldview that included ideologies of democracy and otherworldly theologies, and an endeavor that for the most part did not fully develop or accept native leaders at the same level as missionaries and carried a hidden agenda of Americanization. The disempowering elements in theological education, which were reinforced through the power of the purse, continued until the end of the last century. It leaves a legacy of mission as both the source and the focus of the Latin@ church. Mission has continued to be a strong and important focus for bringing relevance to the gospel message and the embeddedness of the church not only in Latin American cultures but also in other contexts of the Latin American diaspora. When examining the mission and vision statements of different theological institutions in Latin America and the diaspora today, we can see that mission is still a central focus or underlying reason for theological education. With both its strengths and limitations, this history of mission and how it has influenced the formation of leaders in theological education are a starting point. What alternative visions do we have for moving forward? What theological underpinnings could inform these options? The following chapter discusses the central understanding and development of mission for our present times.

2

El Sacerdocio Universal

Preparing a Priesthood of Believers for a Holistic Mission

What has taken place in Latin@ theological education since the early twentieth century? How has the historical legacy of rooting theological education in mission continued or changed? What has occurred as native leadership has developed in the churches? How have these same influences taken on new forms and continued to subdue native leadership? It is clear that theologies of mission continue to be central for the ways churches with roots in Latin America think about theological education. But those theologies of mission have changed over time. In this chapter I will track some of the most important changes in missional theology and explain their significance for theological education. I will discuss three important foundations that need to guide Latin@ theological education: *misión integral*, the good news of the *basileia* of God, and the priesthood of all believers.

Protestantism in Latin America has been a product of missions, and as Latin American clergy became leaders within Protestantism, the churches' identity remained strongly missiological. Over the course of the twentieth century and into the twenty-first century, as civil wars, natural disasters, and the economic implications of trade agreements in Latin America and the Caribbean pushed persons to emigrate, Latin American clergy took with them this missionary impetus, planting new churches across the United States and parts of Europe such as the Netherlands, Spain, and Switzerland. Latin American Protestants have worked not only with their own people groups in these places but also with marginalized groups such as gypsies/Roma in Spain. The theology of the church continues to derive from a sense of mission.

In his work *The Faces of Latin American Protestantism*, José Míguez Bonino observes that the theological principle that best expresses the life and dynamic of the religious community, that gives coherence and consistency to the understanding of the gospel, and that will become a point of reference for the theological building of the Latin American church as a community is mission.[1] He notes that this principle "is not visible as an explicit theological formulation but rather as an 'ethos' that permeates the speech, worship, and life of the Protestant community, a self-understanding manifested in all attitudes, conflicts, and priorities."[2]

Since the World Missionary Conference in Edinburgh in 1910, these theologies of mission have been articulated more explicitly. The Latin American and thus the Latin@ churches have appropriated an ecclesiological missiology based on the sovereignty of Jesus Christ and of the kingdom of God. Its origins were connected to colonialism, but in the last five decades the Latin American church has sought to shape its own ways of doing theology. As leaders have come together to examine their context and the work of the church, they have redefined theology as *misión integral* (integral or holistic mission). This redefinition began in Latin America but emigrated to the United States with the people, taking nuanced expression in accordance with the lived realities of this context. Second-generation leaders, those born in the US context, will diversify the missiological expressions of the church even further. How will this influence the shape of theological education?

Mission is central to the theology of the church—her definition, her meaning, and her purpose in the world. The danger of this theology lies in its potential to create a monopoly of the church over Jesus and the Holy Spirit, which can become as triumphalist as colonial missions. The balance to counteract this has been the "option of the poor" offered by Jon Sobrino's ecclesiology and the emphasis on the "servant Christ" of Emilio Castro's missiology.[3]

Similar to some aspects of more conservative Protestantism in the United States, Protestantism in Latin America has confused evangelization with mission. This means that it has defined the mission of the church as preaching the gospel of salvation of souls and inviting people to a conversion experience. In so doing it has reduced the proclamation of the gospel to the experience of being "born again." Míguez Bonino points out that such an approach "fail[s] to participate in the fullness of the work of the triune God."[4] In the 1970s, René Padilla, Pedro Savage, Samuel Escobar, José Arana, and other Latin American theologians and practitioners began to speak about the fullness of the task of the church, precisely in order to move away from these reduction-ist expressions. These writers included service as justice and social responsibility, a *pastoral approach* that responds to the daily needs of the people. These areas of ministry have been ex-pressions of mainline Christianity, or what is called the *iglesias históricas* (historical churches). But what about newer churches, such as those of the Pentecostals?

It is particularly important to explain how these expressions of justice and social responsibility take place in the Pentecostal community, as Pentecostalism has become the largest expres-sion of Christianity in Latin America and the Caribbean. Pen-tecostalism came to Latin America in the early 1900s. At first, other Protestant Christian leaders greatly criticized Pentecostals. Yet, even after almost half a century of work in Latin America, the mainline churches had not truly been able to penetrate most populations of Latin America. Missionaries had confined their dialogue to the intelligentsia in their attempt to influence the leaders with the hopes that it would trickle down. However, clas-sism did not permit the level of trickle-down they had hoped for or expected. The masses had not been affected by the Protestant Christian movement. Pentecostalism, on the other hand, offered the masses more than religious ritual. It offered an experience of healing and of personal transformation that opened up the

33

horizons of what was possible in one's life, even in the midst of poverty. The work of the Holy Spirit was able to transcend the barriers of their poverty and offered hope, light, and power or strength for daily living. Pentecostalism took root quickly, as believers were trained and thus empowered as leaders in the movement. The understanding of the empowerment of persons via the gifts of the Spirit allowed even the poor to offer help to each other and to feel that contributing something to the community was within their reach. Having the Bible in their own hands and the freedom to interpret the Scriptures through the empowerment of the Spirit equalized the educated and the uneducated, as it was the Spirit who chose without bias to reveal the understanding of the Scriptures. The Spirit and its manifestations gave persons a "certainty of the nearness and living presence of a forgiving and accepting God."[5]

Since the early 1900s, Pentecostal theology has evolved in Latin America as well as among Latin@ Pentecostals in the United States, due to social changes in their different countries, such as the Chilean dictatorship or the crisis of immigration in the United States. The capacity to read these moments through the Spirit has developed in Pentecostals a social conscience, which they express as service to those who are in need—not only toward fellow Pentecostals but much more broadly and inclusively throughout their communities. Pentecostals have institutionalized these efforts, as individual churches or Pentecostal denominations have created nonprofit organizations that offer care to the marginalized, such as a child-care service program created by the Assemblies of God, or La Red, formed by a group of Latin@ pastors to address immigration issues. They have also included advocacy as part of their expression of faith.

Groups of Pentecostals have organized a series of consultations in order to articulate their own Pentecostal experience and understanding and ethical convictions with regards to society. A meeting that took place in Santiago de Chile in 1990 to debate the challenges and contributions of the Pentecostal church in the context of Latin America reflected the new awareness of the church in society. In some of their statements, the group recognized that Pentecostal theology at times offers hope but at other times offers escapism as a solution. It is helpful to quote here a statement from a similar meeting, the Encuentro de Pentecostales Latinoamericanos in 1988:

> We reaffirm our conviction regarding the work of the Holy Spirit, manifested in various gifts; in faith experiences that impact personal life, community life, and all of creation, transforming them and filling them with the fullness of God. Fullness which is shown in the multiform grace of the Lord, in liberating actions of the Spirit which demolish sinful structures of destruction, misery, and death vanquished by Jesus Christ; in the powerful testimonies of men and women who in the church and beyond struggle and work for "the abundant life" promise of Jesus with the poor, the sad, those who have no succor, the oppressed.[6]

We can see in this statement a definition of Pentecostal social conscience taking shape with an accompanying theological articulation that is informed by a Trinitarian understanding and an emphasis on the work of the Holy Spirit in the church that recognizes the structural forms of sin and the authority of Jesus in this realm. This statement articulates the work of the church that expresses a renewed awareness and desire to address the daily dilemmas of the people at both the personal and structural levels.

The theological expressions that have emerged from this pastoral praxis have placed in the limelight the once-marginalized Pentecostal church. Political leaders seeking to ride the church's wave of influence among the masses have recognized Pentecostals. This presents a need for an analytical-critical understanding of the political sphere, for without it honest leaders might be co-opted by ideological options that cannot easily be discerned as being in conflict with the church's values or that produce consequences that have disastrous effects for the people of the church.

An example of such co-optation is how Latin@ Pentecostal groups were duped into believing President Trump was chosen by God, only to find themselves betrayed by the political agenda of the conservative church groups of the dominant culture. The Latin@ church continues to work through the crisis created by the policies of the president that they helped to bring to power through their vote. Latin@s had trusted these conservative white groups because they shared a common theology, but they had not discerned that their sociopolitical needs were at odds with those groups.

This example points to the need to train churches for participation in public life. Such training should include continued theological reflection and articulation that accompany an understanding of the church's place in public life and, in particular, in relationship to certain issues for which they choose to advocate as part of their service and expanded understanding of the mission of the church, issues such as affordable housing, quality education, and immigration. In the United States, as the Latin@ church becomes more second generation, such training could awaken advocacy, community organizing, and political vocations as callings.

This clear sense of mission can become the basis for theological education. The curricula and pedagogies will be based on this ecclesiological and missiological self-understanding of the Latin American and Latin@ church. The dynamic flow of the church in both contexts creates an ongoing shared exchange of ideas and strategies for the development of the church. If we are to reflect critically on our inherited theologies and the colonial roots of our history, and if we are to have a different understanding of ourselves as church and of our sense of meaning and purpose as church—thus of our mission—then it is crucial that we redefine terms such as the "Lordship of Christ," "servanthood," the "kingdom of God," and the "proclamation of the gospel." The broad term for this redefinition is *misión integral*, or "integral mission."

Misión Integral *(Integral or Holistic Mission)*

Misión integral was born out of the self-theologizing of radical evangelical Protestant groups such as Comunidad Internacional de Estudiantes Evangélicos, La Fraternidad Teólogica Latinoamericana, Escuela Biblica de Villa Maria, and Comunidad Kairos. These groups have long been doing theology in a way that responds to their context and from a radical evangelical perspective, with an integral missional intent and a focus on the formation of all Christians through interdisciplinary dialogue, communal design, and implementation.[7] *Misión integral* is a term that communicates the concern for integral or holistic salvation and the need for social change. *Misión integral* has a liberation approach that is deeply contextual.

In her dissertation about the movement that started to define *misión integral* and to craft a theological education that would train persons to implement it, Ruth Padilla Deborst comments that "theologies of liberation and the integral mission movement were concurrent responses to the Latin American context of the times" in and around the 1970s. The Fraternidad Teólogica Latinoamericana (FTL), a group of pastors/theologians from across Latin America, "generated a contextual theology with liberative tools that maintained respect for scriptures while taking praxis seriously. It was an evangelical conservative theology and a radical orientation to faith and society."[8]

Misión integral is a term that is beginning to encapsulate the role of the church in the world as disciples of Christ. It is being used in the Latin American diaspora as well. René Padilla defines a church that seeks to practice *misión integral* as one "in which God's Spirit is free to act so that in it the Word of God becomes flesh."[9] "The kingdom of God becomes the main hermeneutical principle for understanding the gospel, Jesus and the mission of his followers in the world."[10] The community of faith gives priority to the kingdom of God (to which I will refer as the *basileia*)[11] and the Lordship of Christ, practices discipleship as a missionary lifestyle into which all its members have been called, and lives in such a way that it witnesses to the inauguration of a new humanity by using its gifts and ministries to fulfill their "vocations as God's co-workers in the world."[12]

Padilla Deborst sees the *basileia* as neither a territorial realm in the present nor a promised realm that exists only in the future. Instead, she sees it as a dynamic in which the power of God is enacted. It manifests itself through Jesus, and manifests itself in the church by the work of the Holy Spirit through every person by way of the gifts of the Spirit that have been poured out freely upon all, without regard to age, gender, or class. In this realm, Jesus the risen Christ is Lord over everything and everyone and has authority or sovereignty over all creation (Phil. 2:6–11; Eph. 1:22). This Lordship of Christ implies that there is no arena of life in which Jesus is not present or into which he does not call his church. This therefore eliminates all dichotomies such as sacred/secular and spirit/flesh. It opens up all spheres as places for mission. Disciples of Jesus are to carry out this mission. It begins in them as a process of transformation, the goal of which is to re-create in the believer the fullness of the image of Christ, just as the work of the Spirit in the world through the church is to transform the different arenas of life into places where the fullness of the life and justice of Christ is to be expressed. This is the redeeming proclamation of the gospel. This makes the church an agent of love and life through its service as its sign of commitment to Jesus, whom she calls Lord/*Kyrios*. This is what it means to follow Jesus. Padilla Deborst defines this as "a process of transformation lasting a whole lifetime and extending to every aspect of life."[13]

The good news is not information but a dynamic response of the church to the call of Christ to do mission in the world along with him. To do so, all its members are to use their gifts and ministries in the power of the Spirit of God, for it is with these gifts that the Holy Spirit has equipped the church to reflect the love and will of God in all realms of creation. This is the fulfillment of the vocation of each disciple as God's coworker in the world.

The telos is the *basileia* and its justice as a new order of life, not the church and its narrow understanding of evangelization as a message without concrete action.

Jesus and his disciples preached while also healing, liberating, and showing compassion to poor and marginalized people (Matt. 10:7–8; Luke 4:16–19). In the parable of the sheep and the goats, the *basileia* is clearly defined as doing good to the least of these (Matt. 25:31–46). In Pauline writings, the *basileia* is defined as the ministry of reconciliation. The Greek term Paul uses—*katallage*—denotes a change in relationship between individuals, groups, or nations.[14] The ministry of reconciliation takes place because "Christ's love compels us." Elsewhere I have written of how, for Latina *evangélicas*, this compelling love not only drives them to carry out this work but also surrounds and holds them together. The love keeps them from being crushed by the external pressures that come as a result of doing this work.[15] For this work to take place, Christ, through the actions of the Holy Spirit, has equipped us with charisms, which are given so that we may serve the community in love. A doctrine that brings together this sense of ministry and the exercise of the charisms by all is the doctrine of the priesthood of all believers.

The Doctrine of the Priesthood of All Believers

The doctrine of the priesthood of all believers is of prime importance for the life of the church.[16] It accommodates and facilitates the ability of the church to act as the agent of the Holy Spirit on behalf of the *basileia*. This doctrine is based on 1 Peter 2:4–11. These verses give us a New Testament view of the church as the people of God. Verse 9 gives us three terms for defining the people of God: "chosen people," "royal priesthood," and "holy nation." These come from three passages in the Hebrew Scriptures: Exodus 19:5, which describes Israel as a "treasured possession" among all the peoples; Isaiah 43:20, which calls Israel "my people, my chosen"; and Isaiah 61:6, which says, "you will be called priests of the LORD, you will be named ministers of our God."

The new community being formed, founded on the cornerstone Christ, takes on the same honor and names of Israel. The church is the new Israel, and through the work of the Holy Spirit she is the agent of the *basileia* as a part of her mission. This is how the Latin@ church has read and interpreted this passage.

This chosenness can only be understood within the context of mercy: "Once you were not a people, but now you are the people of God; once you had not received mercy, but now you have received mercy" (1 Pet. 2:10). In Christ we have a new closeness or intimacy with God. This privilege comes with the responsibility of obedience. The Exodus 19:5 passage urges us to hear the voice of God; keeping God's covenant is what makes Israel a peculiar treasure. We are chosen to serve. We use our honor to serve. The privilege is that we are chosen and used for the purposes of God, which are fulfilled by way of our obedience as it aligns us with the will of God. To be a royal priesthood means we have access to God through Christ. In Latin the word for priest is *pontifex*, which means a bridge builder. The believer constructs a bridge or a path to Christ by way of the proclamation of an incarnational word. This is our spiritual sacrifice. Our function as the church is to "declare the praises of him who called [us] out of darkness into his wonderful light" (1 Pet. 2:9).

For the most part, during the times of the early fathers of the church, such as Clement, Polycarp, Justin Martyr, Irenaeus, and Cyprian, the laity functioned in the church in accordance with their spiritual gifts. The laity could baptize if there was no priest, they could listen to the confession of a dying person, and they could preach. The church had criteria for those who ministered, similar to what is described in 1 Timothy 3. The "spiritual sacrifices" that the laity could offer included prayers, praise, charity, and the conversion of nonbelievers (evangelistic work). Holy communion—better described in Spanish as *la santa cena*, the holy meal—was a full meal. All would pray for the meal, but the elements were blessed by the priest, and then part of the meal was distributed to the poor. Even though the priest blessed the elements and said the words of institution, that did not separate the priest from the congregation. This lack of separation was one reason why women could play significant leadership roles up to and including the time when Polycarp was bishop. He established the order of widows in the work of the church called the "altar of God." This work of charity was a part of the spiritual sacrifices. Polycarp was not alone in his vision of all believers having priestly duties. Justin Martyr's writings explain that just as Christ is a priest, so too is the whole congregation. Spiritual sacrifices were a corporate expression of that shared priesthood.

During the time of Irenaeus, the trained priests were particularly charged with defending the faith among other thinkers, and for this they used the tools of philosophy. But the church fathers continued to emphasize that all were priests—until the time of Cyprian (195–258), whose ideas were influenced by the political organizations of Rome. Cyprian's ideas about the supervision of ecclesial bodies were similar to those of the Roman Empire, in which each province had a supervisor of the religion of the state. Later, when Constantine converted to Christianity, the role of the supervisor of the religion of the state became that of the Christian bishop. At this point, all rites for entrance into the church and continuation in the life of the church depended on the bishop. Cyprian writes: "the bishop is in the church and the church is in the bishop."[17] These words constitute a new thing: the special authority of the priest. This authority, which once resided in the congregation as a whole, from this point on resided only in the person of the official priest. A priestly order had emerged. The sacrifice offered is only that of the passion of Christ, and it is offered only by the priest. The royal priesthood no longer refers to a people but to a special class of priests.

At this time in the history of the church, it was necessary to unite the church around its doctrines, and Cyprian placed the responsibility of uniting the church and of guarding the doctrine in the office of the bishop. The bishop was in charge of guarding the peace and unity of the church in order to avoid schisms. Now the bishop alone had special functions and tasks, ones that had once belonged to all. From these special functions flows the idea of special powers.

The bishop initiated persons into the church through baptism and the confirmation of baptism. Only the bishop could lay hands on the baptizand or confirmand and officiate at the Eucharist, bringing believers into communion with Christ. This forms a new priestly order that emanates from the idea of apostolic succession. The words of Jesus to Peter, "On this rock I will build my church" (Matt. 16:18), which were once applied to all Christians, were interpreted in a new light and applied only to the priestly order. The Holy Communion was called the sacrament of the sacrifice of the Lord, and the authority to officiate over it resided in the bishop because it was the bishop who did as Christ taught and acted. The other spiritual sacrifices are not mentioned.

Writing in the late fourth and early fifth century, Augustine placed some checks and balances on these new interpretations and preached the offering of oneself as a living sacrifice. Saint Gregory Palamas believed such a sacrifice could only be offered by the persons themselves, so that in this sense individual people are their own priests. People can be their own priests in matters of the purification of the soul, in participation in the mission of the universal church, and in coming to the knowledge of God. Long after Augustine, during the medieval era, other friars, monks, and mystics developed theologies that contributed to the restoration of the ideas of the doctrine of the priesthood of all believers. But over time, this became a minority report. The institutional church increasingly consolidated spiritual powers in the hands of a distinct priestly class.

In the sixteenth century, Martin Luther enumerated seven marks of the church: the preaching of the Word, baptism, Holy Communion, Christian discipline and forgiveness, the call and the consecration to Christian ministry, discipleship, and the cross (meaning the many forms of suffering through which the church must pass).

Luther addressed a church that had a limited understanding of the grace of God. Within that perspective, grace is not the favor of

God expressed in the gospel or the Word. Instead, it is a supernatural power contained in the sacraments. As such, it is not necessary that grace be related to faith, since this supernatural power does not need the faith of the believer to be enacted but is mediated by a transforming supernatural power and therefore requires an authority and power to be mediated to others. The limited, clericalist understanding is that this power was only bestowed on Peter and his apostolic successors—the priestly class. For Luther, by contrast, preaching and Holy Communion communicate the gospel and awaken the soul to a response of faith. As such, when we respond to this faith, we are incorporated into the body of Christ— the church. The body of Christ is the result of the proclamation of the Word. The ministry is located within the body of Christ. The grace of God is expressed in the gospel. Where there is faith in the gospel, there is a church that listens to the gospel. For Luther, faith and the gospel go hand in hand. If they become separate, the church easily goes from being the body of Christ to being merely a social club. Because the ministry is located within the body of Christ, we have a chosen people and the priesthood of all believers rather than a priestly class in the church.

The final outcome of the proclamation of the Word and the administration of the sacraments is to unite the believer with God and to unite the priests with the laity so that both are equal. There is no hierarchy in the church; only Christ is the head of the church. Unity with God is through faith in Jesus, and it is the Holy Spirit who does the work of salvation in our lives. For Luther, this equality between priest and laity was important because it granted all people the same access to God. If only one person can make the grace of God accessible to the others, then that one can also deny access to others. However, when faith in the Word and the work of the Spirit is what provides access to grace, when grace is distributed and all can receive it, then there is no exception of persons. When it comes to service, such ministry is understood to occur not only within the church but also in the world.

We need but two things to be faithful servants in this understanding of the priesthood of all believers. The first is vocation.

All must be provided opportunities to discover their vocation, and then opportunities to develop that vocation. The second thing we need to know is the state of the world. We need to inform ourselves about the state of the world in order to be moved through the Spirit to use our vocation for the restoration and redemption of the world.

Understanding the brokenness of the world and its corruption helps us to deepen our understanding of the proclamation of the Word, since the state of the world prompts us to ask new questions in light of that Word. These questions deepen the faith. Understanding faith in the context of the world allows us to use our faith to carry out our vocation. Faith lived within the context of the world determines the diversity of needs and the vocations that can be developed to address these needs by the ministries of the priesthood of all believers.

The common calling of our priesthood is to serve. What is of prime interest is the calling and not the status. We respond to our callings because of the grace of God to us, and therefore we give by grace what we have received by grace. It is this grace from God and this calling by grace that equalize priests and laity in both the privilege and the responsibility of our calling. Neither clergy nor laity is a class of lords. The ministry of the clergy is given by Christ to the church as a gift so that the Word is preached and the sacraments are administered. Ordination is a public confirmation of that calling, and at ordination the person ordained does not receive special power but rather a commissioning.

The Priesthood of All Believers and the Ministry of the Latin@ Church

Why is this important to the understanding of the ministry of the Latin@ church and to theological education? The doctrine of the priesthood of all believers as revived by Martin Luther showed the way to break from the medieval hierarchical structure of the church. Luther reinterpreted the biblical notion of the universal priesthood by reaffirming that all Christians become priests through their baptism in Christ.[18] For the Latin@ ecclesial community, that has become a practical way to fulfill the mission of the church. For Latin American theologians, it has been the way to bring the church to the fulfillment of an enfleshed mission.

This understanding of mission coupled with the priesthood of all believers has great consequences for how authority is exercised in the church. Latin American theologians have placed the responsibility of governing the church in the hands of all Christians. This does away with the specialized vocations of the clergy and empowers all Christians at every level of the church. In many countries, this is a way of breaking away from the colonized understandings of the missionaries and the paralyzing grip of dictatorships. In the United States, it empowers those who have no status as citizens or who are discriminated against in society.

However, while the Pentecostal church has used the gifts of the Spirit to empower the laity, ministerial power in the ecclesial structure is still carried out in a more traditional, authoritarian way. Such power depends on the minister having access to the charism of leadership, and leaders have many times been exalted as having a special, even exclusive, authority from God. The authority and power of society are reflected in the church and rationalized by theological/biblical means, thus distorting and limiting the fullness of Pentecost. In his book *Ecclesiogenesis: The Base Communities Reinvent the Church*, Leonardo Boff describes the charism of presiding as the gift that brings "unity of the whole to the order and harmony of the charisms, in such wise that all things will work together for the upbuilding of the same body. . . . This will be the charism of assistance, of direction, of administration (1 Cor. 12:28). . . . The specific formality of the charism does not reside in accumulation and absorption, but in integration and coordination. This charism is within the community and not over it but for the good of the community."[19]

If we change our understanding of church from being an entity to being a dynamic reality—something that happens, an event or the Word of God that must be enfleshed for its full proclamation to take place—it changes these notions of authority.

The proclamation and mission of the church are then seen to take place through the fullness of the diverse gifts of the Spirit enfleshed in each member of the body of Christ, the church. In this way, the gifts of mercy of a woman are as much an extension of the work of Christ in the world as the work of a bishop or an apostle.

In order for the church to respond to the fullness of the work of Christ in the world by seeking to respond to the needs of the community, it must return to a lived understanding of its corporal nature. By remembering the Lordship of Jesus and submitting to his Lordship, the church carries out her diverse vocations in the many spheres of the world of which Jesus is Lord. This also has implications for understanding that the gifts of the Spirit listed in 1 Corinthians 12, Romans 12, and Ephesians 4 are not exhaustive, as Jesus's work in the world must take the forms necessary in each historical time. The gifts of the Spirit will take the forms of grace and wisdom necessary in the world according to the needs of the world. The dichotomies (sacred/secular, body/spirit, church/world) that have kept the church from ministering the fullness of the grace of God in the world no longer have a theological basis because of this shift to understanding that there are many gifts given to many people for the fullness of the work of the Spirit, to understanding the diversity of vocations for responding through ministry to the brokenness in the world, and to understanding the complete authority of Christ in all dimensions of the world. The telos is the vision of the *basileia*. The *basileia* integrates all aspects of life. A praxis of integration is needed between the disciplines and the professions that emerge from these different aspects of life. This implies that it is the Christians within those disciplines and professions and within all of life's activities, reflecting on the places where the Holy Spirit is calling, and acting within those different activities taking place amidst the whole of life's activities, who are the ones to come into a theology of mission that encompasses the understanding of the *basileia* in their midst. Discernment that helps persons to follow the Spirit's calling while unmasking the spirit of death and the actions needed to become instruments of God's life leads to a theology of mission for life and to a process of daily allegiance (praise) to Jesus, the Lord of the *basileia*. In this lies our faithful expression of love to God and neighbor. This is the direction and the purpose of theological education. It is *misión integral* coupled with the practice of the priesthood of all believers that moves us in this direction.

In the next chapter we will begin to imagine the forms theological education that is oriented toward this purpose might take.

3

Notas Pedagógicas

Many Ways to Contextualize Curriculum

In the 1990s, when I began to work as an instructor at different Bible institutes, I found that much of the curriculum was based on the classical disciplines of theological education. Many times we used translations of books written as far back as the 1950s, books that spoke of matters far from the realities of my students. They assumed that abstract theological concepts and historical knowledge about the church would traverse the times, cultures, and generations and would accomplish the same purpose for all groups—to prepare them for ministry. This I found not to be the case. Students read the information and brought questions to it that were far from how the concepts were explained, and the historical material did not allow the students to see where they factored into the church. I found myself using materials that not only represented more current scholarship but were also written by authors from different racial and ethnic contexts who understood the particular context of ministry that my students were engaging. Theology and history from that perspective came alive for my students. It was not just material to memorize but a resource with which to think theologically in light of their particular mission and contexts.

I brought this to the attention of the directors of the Bible institutes, who informed me that this curriculum was a denominational mandate and that, as directors, they had no way of changing it. Furthermore, they insisted, it was important that students be tested on this (outdated) material and not on the extracurricular aspects I was bringing to the classroom. It took a while to convince them that my material was biblically and theologically sound. What counted as necessary knowledge for ministry had been prescribed by others. In some cases, the directors were simply replicating their own theological education experiences, and the curriculum they were asking me to use had been part of that experience. In the interests of their students, instructors like me intuitively contextualized the materials in class discussions. Out of deference to the directors, we presented summaries of the assigned text materials and exams that reflected our understanding of these materials. In the classroom discussions, we contextualized and supplemented the prescribed materials. But this was not a formal, stated goal of the institute. In most cases, the Bible institute curriculum sought to ensure that so-called sound doctrine was transmitted, not that it was relevant to the students.

This way of engaging curriculum not only created a sense of powerlessness, it also fostered among the participants a sense of living in two worlds: a world of the powers that decided the curriculum, and a world of ministry to the students by instructors who bring to the classroom their ministry experience and their wisdom from the context of their everyday lives. The formal material was *embotellado*, bottled up for the exam, but the true learning occurred in significant conversations and the imparting of wisdom by teachers who had much ministry experience, when these were to be found at the institutes. This ministry and theological knowledge was transmitted to the contexts of ministry. Yet it was not written down, and therefore it was limited to the sphere of influence of the students of a particular instructor or institute.

This experience prompts the question: What is an empowering curriculum for Latin@ ministry? *Protestant ?*

Before answering that, I want to define briefly the different types of curricula. The official or formal curriculum, or the overt or stated curriculum, consists of the courses, lessons, and learning activities in which students participate, as well as the knowledge and skills that educators intentionally teach the students. The hidden or unofficial curriculum is the unwritten and implicit lessons, values, and academic, social, and cultural messages that are communicated to students while they are in school. In theological education, that curriculum may be communicated by who is included or excluded in the required reading versus the suggested reading for students. The implicit curriculum reflects the deepest values of the school, whether or not those values line up with the values expressed in its formal, public policies. The absent or null curriculum or the excluded curriculum is that which is not taught at all. Sometimes the teacher or the system ignores some content, voices, or skill, deliberately or unwittingly. A teacher may consider some idea unimportant and ignore it. Identifying these different types of curricula at our schools is an important exercise for the directors, faculty, and boards.

Does your curriculum really reflect your school's values? What is missing from it? Why?

Curriculum and Contextualized Theology

Having previously discussed the theological construct that guides the mission of the churches, we now look at options for curricular expressions that will equip leaders for ministry. What are the layers of ideologies that underlie the theologies as well as the diversity of knowledges that inform these theological frameworks? I show how these theological frameworks can create contradictions that have tended to separate different congregations and *concilios*.[1] These separations have thwarted congregations' efforts to find common spaces for partnering in the ministry. The generational knowledges that are based on different perspectives of the current *vivencias*, or lived experiences, have kept us from passing the baton of ministry down through the generations. The points of contradiction and the generations meet at the definition of curriculum. In the midst of this diversity and contradiction, I begin to find commonalities by looking at the importance of context. How does our context inform our curricular decisions? Is the theology of *misión integral* on our radar as we make curricular decisions? How is this a discernment process about our mission?

Orlando E. Costas reminds us that context is important in the church's understanding of her faith and mission in the world. Attention to context makes the life-in-mission of the church more relevant. This also affects theology, for it "stems from the peculiar situation in which Christians find themselves." Theology must engage the present historical moment of the church so that theology is "reflection on the faith in the light of one's historical context."[2] Context is the surrounding conditions, setting, and environment in which something exists. It is a reality in time and space that ties together and shapes all knowledge.[3] Knowledge can only exist and be generated in and from a contextual reality.

Such an understanding of theology steers us away from theology as *sana doctrina* (sound doctrine)—a set of universal formulations that cannot be changed and that comes from outside of ourselves to define us, regardless of our present situation and culture.[4] This also changes the epistemology, pedagogy, and curriculum because it steers us away from a taught transmissive theology and from being inactive recipients of that transmission. Instead it situates us as agents who are actively engaged in a collaborative construction of knowledge. Since this knowledge is contextual, it is also practical. "It is human sensorial activity, shaped by reality and geared toward its transformation."[5] Therefore, in a theological teaching/learning setting, we understand the elements of this context in relationship to one another and to God in the contextual history. The elements include ideas, values, attitudes, experiences, feelings, and our interpretations of these. We share these interpretations of reality with one another.

The context is likewise a fluid reality. The process of interpreting the Scripture while also considering the context places us in a zone of transformation where the past, the present, and the challenge of the future all intersect with the gospel. This reflects the nature of God and God's revelation history. For God is contextual, and the accounts in the Scriptures reveal a God who is bound by culture, language, and symbols that are contextual. In the incarnation, God reveals Godself through the Son Jesus and becomes "the Word of life" (1 John 1:1), and "reflects the glory of God and bears the very stamp of his nature" (Heb. 1:3 RSV). This confirms that the nature of God is contextual and that bearing witness to this gospel is a contextual matter. Theology, therefore, is a contextual discipline; it interprets God in the light of the life and ministry of Jesus Christ. Rather than being absent from our history and from suffering, Jesus came and continues to come to us to break the chains of the oppressive forces that cause suffering. Christ is present in the person and ministry of the Holy Spirit, an extension of the incarnation. The church represents the risen Christ in and through its mission, and is called through that mission to give witness to this contextual Christ by incarnating him in the church's respective situations of oppression.[6] For this work, the ministries of the church must be "immersed in the concrete situations of the disenfranchised and witness to the lordship and saviorhood of Christ . . . a commitment which will be verified in our participation in the concrete transformation of these situations."[7] This is the work of ministry of the church for which theological education equips all the members of the body of Christ, the priesthood of all believers. This vision informs the content of our curriculum, our pedagogy, and our doing of theology.

Our ideologies underlie our theologies and therefore influence them. Our ideology is manifested in and by our shared beliefs, attitudes, and behaviors. These take form in our social practices such as family rules, relationships, and institutional life. Ideologies create the horizon of ideas and significations through which we filter reality. Our values and our understanding of money, of relationships, and of how human beings are to be seen and treated stem from our ideologies.

To transform an ideology, one needs to generate a new consciousness, that is, the ideas and understandings that echo through our minds and make up the foundational thinking for our sense of purpose and motivation. When people share a consciousness, a sense of meaning and purpose in life, they are able to mobilize in accordance with the beliefs and values that make up that purpose, including developing critical movements or mobilization that requires group action and practices for engaging one's energy in ways that reinforce a different ideology and that have the goal of creating change in an unjust system.

Generating a new consciousness involves coming to an awareness of the cultural blinders and ideological filters through which we interpret the world. It also involves creating experiences of enough depth, duration, and intensity that the prevailing interpretations can be transformed. When this takes place, we increase the possibility of fostering power that promotes God's purposes for sufficiency, solidarity, and emancipation. This power may be expressed by our theology. This is what we hope can take place by way of the curriculum of theological education that has as its purpose an integrated mission of the church. An integrated mission includes preaching, teaching, liturgy or worship, fellowship, social action or service, and prophetic ministry in the community, or social justice. It includes the disciplines that give us the tools for a more excellent practice of these areas. For example, for social justice we need to understand how to organize communities, how to write grants, and what are the different areas for economic development, among other things. What would it take for a theological education curriculum to have this as its core purpose?

Curriculum and Knowledge: Creating Our Own Curriculum

Thinking theologically about curriculum requires being attuned to the many different kinds of knowledge involved in faithful Christian living. I begin with a working definition of curriculum that I shall expand as I continue this reflection.

Religious educator Robert Pazmino defines curriculum as "the vehicle or medium through which educational vision takes root in the actual content being offered."[8] This content includes several dimensions, such as the affective, the rational, and the behavioral. To these I add relational knowledge, knowledge from dreams and the imagination, and spiritual knowledge.

Figure 1. Types of Knowledge

Knowledge Dimension & Description	Curriculum Telos	Praxis (Examples)
Rational Knowledge: the capacity to gather, organize	To use the information	To analyze situations
Creative Knowledge: the capacity to remember, to connect to the present and the future	To imagine	To create
Affective (Heart) Knowledge: the capacity to feel; growth in feelings or emotional areas	To feel, to discern emotions. To recognize contradictions and confusion.	To influence learning and depth of inquiry. To gain clarity about power relations
Dream Knowledge: the subconscious dimension that gives us the capacity to construct a vision	To open up to us the subconscious dimension where all is possible and real and the seemingly bizarre is the key to interpretation. God speaks to us in symbols and images or narrative.	Knowledge to construct a vision

Spiritual (Spirit) Knowledge: the capacity to access higher values, meaning, and purpose of life	Energy for purpose in life. Connects us with all living entities.	Deeper understanding of our interdependence with those who at first may seem different than we are
Holistic Knowledge: the capacity that helps us to be aware of how the different dimensions of knowledge are connected	To see connections between different types of knowing	Integration

The first type of knowledge is rational knowledge. This is the intellectual capacity to gather, organize, and use information in order to analyze situations. Second is creative knowing, or the capacity to remember, imagine, and create. It is the premonition of ideas. Such knowledge prompts us to ask, "What can I do with this information?" Third, heart knowledge is the capacity to feel. The emotions affect the quality of our interactions and work and influence learning and the depth of inquiry. Being able to discern emotions helps us to recognize contradictions and confusion and to gain clarity about power relations. This is important, for we often underestimate the conflicts and contradictions that can take place when we are encountering others or attempting to create community.

Dreams and imagination are a fourth dimension of knowledge. The Western world, with its understanding of the Enlightenment, has trouble with this one, but those of us who did not go through the passageway of the Enlightenment have found dreams to be a rich source of knowing—the kind of knowing that opens up to us the subconscious dimension where all is possible and real and the seemingly bizarre is the key to interpretation. It is the place where God speaks to us in symbols and images or narrative. Dreams give us knowledge; they help shape a vision.

Spirit knowledge is the fifth dimension. This is the capacity to be and to have energy for purpose in life. It connects us with all living entities and allows us to come to a deeper understanding of our interdependence with others whom we may at first perceive to be different from ourselves. Sixth and finally there is holistic knowing, which both helps us see the connections between the different types of knowing and integrates them all.[9]

The doing of theology has its starting point in these different kinds of knowledge. When we come to the table with a diversity of knowledges, then we find contradictions. In a fluid reality such as immigration, we have the opportunity to find common spaces in the midst of the contradictions. This place may be a prophetic space of grace that particularly permits the construction of hope.[10]

Education and Shifting Perspective

The process of education can be a space for shifts in perspective. The more disciplines included in the process of education, the greater the number of lenses through which we learn to look at reality. In theological education, we create not only courses but opportunities to be in service with others who are from our church world as well as from a variety of different worlds living in the same community, thus suffusing the process with different knowledges. In such a context, we can expand the theological reflection and ask wider missiological questions when we look at the work of God in the world—the *missio Dei*.

In a conversation with a young Latina pastor in New York City, I realized how important such multiperspectival theological reflection is. She is tasked with revitalizing an aging congregation that after years of neglecting its building now needs to raise about $400,000 to make the space functional once more. While seeking the funds, she has had fruitful conversations with community partners who are carrying out a variety of important services in the community. Those conversations have helped them to understand how together they can form an ecology of services in the community, which has a common goal of eradicating the poverty in the community through different means of empowerment. While not all can openly express a faith-based vision, they can share sufficient common values to base empowerment on a dignified treatment of all persons. God is at work through these values and the many ways of empowerment of the people: education, entrepreneurship, legal aid, financial literacy, and housing.

The curriculum is a design that includes the organization of the multitude of experiences that the teacher, along with the students, bring to a common space of collaborative dialogue. The dialogue will spark new interpretations, which help to transform the life of the participants, their communities, systems, and structures. These experiences and dialogue will give them access to the accumulated wisdom for theological reflection and ministerial praxis. This wisdom is made up of the diverse knowledges and content that are a part of the dialogue.

Globalization as the Context of Dialogue for Ministry Knowledge

What is the context in which this dialogue takes place? There are as many contexts as there are cultures, loci, and subcultures of the different generations that live together in our communities and attend our churches. How then can one best describe the context of ministry? Is there a common category that can be used to define that context? I suggest globalization as a principal feature of reality in our present time. The forces of globalization affect every community and society in the world. The understandings of globalization that come from Wati Longchar, who was a consultant for Ecumenical Theological Education based in northeast India, can be helpful for our discussion. Globalization refers to the opening up of national boundaries to international trade and global competition. On the one hand, this opens up opportunities that can enhance the lives of persons in countries that produce fewer goods or have less access to goods that can improve the quality of life. Technology, as an important part of these features, has brought about an exchange of ideas between persons throughout the globe that largely has been mutually beneficial.

Yet such economic expressions of globalization are typically controlled by the richer countries. Those richer countries determine the processes of development and do not take into consideration the needs of the poorer nations that provide the labor of production, the land, and the products. These matters are controlled by the goals of the multinational companies, typically goals of growth that often reflect greed rather than need. Foreign trade and the attendant conditions of loans are not determined by the developing countries and smaller entrepreneurs who cannot survive in a market skewed to the interests of those who can buy and sell on a dime in response to the patterns of consumption of the rich. "The opening of the national boundaries for [a] free market has led to a neo-colonialism allowing not only economic domination but political domination over the poor countries. The International Monetary Fund (IMF) . . . and World Bank have created conditions that have weakened the states and made the IMF a tool of the rich and powerful."[11] Many governments use their power to suppress the resistance of the poor when they organize to demand a more just system.

The consumerist values propagated by this system make the poor see themselves as backward because they cannot afford the goods and lifestyles of the West. The ecological balance is also affected by unfettered materialism so that the ability of the earth to sustain life is taxed and destroyed. The further marginalization and exclusion of people groups already on the margins are intensified and lead to migration, as persons seek ways of sustaining their lives. Yet such migration/immigration may continue to position them as rightless workers in an urban setting or in a different society. Their situation is exacerbated by those who consider religions to pertain only to the private and personal realm of people's lives and not to a community's sense of shared social responsibility.

Given these realities of globalization, we need to address and integrate into the curriculum areas of knowledge that heretofore have been outside of the traditional theological education curriculum, and listen to voices that can give us insights about these aspects of life. Such areas include globalization, ethnic identity, immigration, and technology.

Presently, theological education is compartmentalized and restricted to disciplines that do not represent the actual complexity of the world and the type of problem solving and analysis needed in our multicultural societies. Today's ministry considerations are typically uninformed by the expertise of the specialized disciplines of economics, social analysis, and action research. To equip church leaders—by which I mean the full priesthood of all believers—we need to develop both interdisciplinary content and pedagogy. Such interdisciplinarity makes the necessary connections between the specialized disciplines and theological reflection. Missing from our teaching and learning are also the perspectives and wisdom of marginalized groups. However, to include a perspective in the curriculum does not mean merely adding a reading, a unit, or a course. A perspective is a lens through which we look at the whole. It helps us to "discover an alternative view of life and vision of human bond to one another."[12] The best outcome of such an interdisciplinary and incarnational perspective occurs when it is fully integrated into our teaching and theological research rather than being a mere add-on.

We must do this to avoid a divorce between the academic world and the lived realities of the communities in which we have our churches. Yet we also want to avoid reducing theological education to teaching Sunday school.[13] In order for praxis thinking to take place, theological education cannot be merely skills oriented any more than it can be solely an intellectual exercise in abstraction. Theory and practice must go hand in hand as we do social cultural analysis of our context that has as its purpose transformation. We must also consider inclusivity when looking at the content of curriculum. The Latinx community, for example, is very diverse. This diversity is a reflection of the Creator, who does not exclude in God's structure of creation but rather affirms diversity. For our part, to affirm diversity, we must welcome the variety of cultures and their theological resources and express them in our curriculum.

Recently, I taught a class of Latinx students from six different countries and three generations. We began by telling each other who we were and what had been the predominant influences in our lives, and how that had played out in our understandings of the work of the church and in our own spiritual hungers. From there we established the values and the rules that would guide our engagement in the classroom. We had to learn to listen very intently and to ask questions of clarification even when we thought we knew what was being discussed. Many times we discovered that our assumed understandings were incorrect, which led to deeper conversation about the matter. Our theologies were different, and this led to heated discussion; when we realized this was not always productive, we asked how we came to believe such things. The question led us to the historical origins of our theological acquisition. Not everyone welcomed this step, for it could have revealed that theology was not always as pure and certain as some desired. The unraveling of such a holy thing was difficult. It became necessary to ask overarching questions that helped us get at deeper understandings of God. These questions came from our contexts and lived realities and the understandings of God and the Scriptures that informed these. To get there, we had to share our deep experiences with God and our knowledge of God. We were reconstructing our understandings and doing theology together while holding each other's souls so as to ensure that we all managed to navigate this passageway without getting lost or being left behind. Recognizing and speaking about this candidly with one another created an intentionality and a genuine sense of caring. In this process we chose readings different from the ones originally noted in the syllabus, readings that addressed the questions and needs of the group in the moment. Participants as well as instructors could name other resources. The values and outcomes of the curriculum rather than the details were the primary operating principles.

Curriculum is not only books or lectures; it also includes the persons involved in the teaching/learning engagement and the content of their lives and realities. The approaches to teaching and presenting and the choice of content and format together create the values upon which curriculum is constructed, as the process of theological education seeks to give us ways to discern what is just and to make ways of justice with the oppressed. Theological education brings us to the work of reconciliation of human bonding and of connecting with creation. Therefore, it integrates aspects of "overcoming violence and peace-making, ecumenism, interfaith dialogue, theoretical and pastoral voices from women, indigenous people, people living with disabilities and other minority oppressed groups."[14] These topics are brought up by the curiosity of participants in the classroom, as a result of their engagement with persons and pastoral dilemmas, and because the instructor suggests that they have been missing as a part of the dialogue—and the students agree. The journeys of immigration and diasporic living become a part of the content of our curriculum. The politics, economics, suffering, structures of new identity formation, and strategies of survival and justice of such immigration and diasporic living must be included if resilience is to open a door to the doing of a theology of hope and thriving that informs an ecclesiology and missiology for the Latin@ community of the diaspora.

Pedagogical Notes and Practices

Fernando Torres Millan writes that "Popular education is education as a practice (or praxis) of freedom. It is an approach to education where participants engage each other and the educator as co-learners to critically reflect on the issues in their community and then take action to change them."[15] Millan is professor at the Dimensión Educativa in Bogota, Colombia. He writes about a model of popular education that is carried out as theological education at popular Bible schools, which are sought out by those who thirst to study the Scriptures. He describes theological education in this context as dialogical education in which the teacher's first movement is listening to the gestures, silences, different opinions, and voices of the students.

For the students, the reading of their reality comes through listening to their culture. Such reading generates a diversity of opinions, as each student reads the world differently. Listening is the starting point in the production of knowledge between persons in the classroom. Teachers listen first so as not to reject the knowledge of the people as erroneous or lacking. Millan likens this to how Jesus listened to the people, after which he asked a question or told a parable that required persons to do critical analysis of their situation. The outcome of this exchange was a new interpretation of the reality in which the hearers found themselves. The wisdom of the Sophia of God is present in this listening. Such listening to or reading of the present is where persons can find the places of suffering and joy of life. This is where they analyze the problems of life and generate new interpretations. Such analysis creates new information and categories and challenges one to consider points of view different from those held previously. Though not accessible prior to this analysis, once accessible, the new information is constructed on the basis of existing knowledge. This dialogical process yields an interpretive collaboration and a willingness of people to consider new things because they are based on what is already familiar to them. This is important for all learners but especially for persons who, for a variety of reasons, are in a process of dislocation (migration/immigration, loss, new place in society) from that which is familiar to them.

These people are able to understand their lives in this new locus through the dialogue and interpretation of the Scriptures. Because it is a dialogical process and persons are free to re-create their lives in light of the Scriptures, persons see what they could not see before about the construction of their lives, about God in their lives. There is also the space to lament if necessary. Lamenting is also a process of leaning into the pain of life and learning about its causes and about who God is and isn't in the midst of that pain. Such discernment enables persons to recognize the difference between the sin of injustice and a spiritual trial for growth. Approached through such discernment, injustice is not spiritualized away into religious categories. Instead, it can enable persons to reinterpret the tradition. They have the tools to make distinctions and interpretations which have an impact on their daily lives. Their new knowledge and information become a way of organizing life problems differently. This pedagogical method is based on Jesus's discussion with the disciples on the road to Emmaus (Luke 24:13–35). The teaching of the Word of God has a transformative effect by bringing students from what is to what can be in their lives. It helps them to prioritize and interpret their problems so as to find solutions not recognized prior to that moment.

The busy lives of persons who are poor or have migrated often do not allow them to extract wisdom from their experiences or reflect on them. Creating a teaching/learning space to intersect the life experience with the practical wisdom, theological reflection, research, knowledge, and skill from the disciplines makes theological education a fertile space. I want to offer three examples of this.

The first takes place in a midsized city in the northeast United States where the context was hard for ministry and the average time a pastor remained was eighteen months to three years. The pastors from this context would come to the workshops and conferences that the Orlando E. Costas Hispanic and Latin-American Ministries Program offered seeking something but not knowing exactly what. Those of us on the teaching and planning staff did not want to say, "Here, this is what you need." Instead, we designed a process whereby the pastors could learn by reflecting on their experiences and hopefully on the direction of their ministries. We designed movements of reflection in groups of three to five pastors each. The first movement invited pastors who had been in the United States for one to three years to speak about their personal experiences. They told stories of discrimination, of the consequences of the language barrier, of racism, of the hardships of being poor, of the violence of their communities, of the unacceptable quality of food in the stores, of inadequate services in their communities—especially in terms of education for their children. They told of the effects these issues and incidents had on them and on their families, of the things they had learned that could stabilize their lives a bit, of the angers and hopeless places of their journey.

As they told these things, a variety of emotions came to the surface—anger and sadness—and even some weeping, because they had not had the opportunity to voice these things or to hear themselves reflect on them previously. We wrote all these things on newsprint.

Then came the second group, which included pastors who had been in the United States three to seven years. We asked them to describe their ministries, the weekly calendar of their churches, and the vision they had for the year. These descriptions were all very similar yet with different emphases. They included full weekly activities of prayer, Bible study, and worship services. Amidst these activities they engaged in evangelism, social action activities, and personal work, that is, a layperson's particular way of sharing his or her witness with others in the community, by going door to door, distributing religious tracts, visiting someone in need or a new believer, or helping a new mother. Women do a lot of such personal work. In some contexts, these activities are named mercy ministries. For example, one church's mercy ministry emphasized visitation in hospitals and prisons.[16] Besides this, the pastors shared their sermon topics, pastoral strategies for growing the church, spiritual formation and discipleship, evangelism—everything they thought was important to share. Also, one church had a Bible institute for discipling purposes and lay ministry preparation. All these elements we also wrote down on newsprint. The long lists of things on both pieces of newsprint were broken up into categories that the pastors named.

The next move was to compare the points of the first group with those of the second group, and to ask how the notes from the two groups related to each other. The pastors studied both lists and wrote down their observations in silence. After that, we asked them to discuss their notes in groups. A slow murmur emerged, but group discussion did not take off. The facilitator discerned a sudden sense of sadness in the room. One pastor broke out into confession and admitted that the first list of experiences and needs was not at all addressed by his practice of ministry. Another pastor comforted him and said, "*No estas solo en esto mi hermano*" (You are not alone in this, my brother). The sadness reflected a sense of shame, and the silence emerged from the inability to face one another in the midst of this reality. They could have chosen to put on a mask and to speak from places of resistance to the truth before them or to project anger upon the facilitators for a process that had not yielded solutions, but instead they chose confession. This was due to the fellowship that had been cultivated among them. *Koinōnia* is an important prelude to these movements.

The next question was: "Why do you think that there is a disconnect between the experiences of our lives and the programs and sermons?" The group was encouraged to see this as a moment to move past shame and to identify problems and find solutions. A rich discussion ensued about how their previous experience of ministry and their theology did not help them since it did not include the categories or issues with which they were dealing now. Their theology was too limited. The pastors recognized that they were dealing with problems they had never encountered in their home countries, problems such as racism. New ways to do ministry were needed as well as new tools and ideas or visions. Together we constructed a list of the gaps and tools needed for ministry in this new situation.

The fourth move now took place. A third group of ministers who had been in the United States longer than ten years and had started to work in new ways shared their ideas, their failures, their frustrations, the partners they had found along the way, and their theological reflections on all these things. Like the previous two groups, they also talked about their fears of sharing new theological thoughts, since some of them had not been well received in other circles. They had been willing to take a risk on this occasion. The energy in the room picked up; they received hearty applause, questions that led to the expansion of the ideas presented, how-tos and funny stories about their trials and errors. The laughter in the room created freedom to play and ask all types of questions without fear. The dialogue was no longer about proving oneself but was now about listening to God in the new ideas and about ways of understanding who God is in this new context and ministry.

What resulted was a strong camaraderie based on support for trying out new things, a list of topics and methods for discussion, and the request that the staff offer future conferences, workshops, and programs. This eventually led to a set of courses that formed part of a degree program in which the participants invited each other to engage with some of their key lay leaders, since most of them were bivocational. The curriculum included retreats for doing theology, out of which new practices for ministry emerged. Through all of this, a fellowship developed that sustained them in ministry, and they remained in their place of ministry for a longer period of time.

The teaching/learning space continued to be a place of discovery, sharing, and theological reflection. Developing a fellowship and place for personal and spiritual development was an important part of the learning experience. The fellowship was important for trying out new things and for daring to go where their theology—*la sana doctrina*—had not gone before. It included a mix of persons in the ministry, from the newcomers to those who had been in the context longer than ten years. Sharing wisdom of ministry across this span of years was important.

Perspective transformation requires support. New insights and their theological implications must be a shared endeavor. Among communal cultures, if one ventures too far from the communal consensus, one may be left outside of that group. For a pastor, in some cases it means becoming irrelevant or being ostracized. If a community of faith decides to follow their pastor into unchartered waters, the entire community must be ready to be considered strange or even suspect by other congregations in the community, denomination, or movement. If, however, there is a fellowship of pastors reflecting on and testing similar new things, as they come to new perspectives they can deepen and expand the tradition together and feel safe doing so.

Textbooks to accompany this type of learning and these kinds of new topics include shorter readings such as articles and chapters. The time needed to invest in shorter readings is more realistic in a bivocational context. The pastors' own writing and research were done in class rather than at home. They were creating projects, sermons, and visions for their congregations that were informed by their pastoral theology. These were things that they could use immediately in their ministries. Researching, writing, and thinking together in the classroom were all forms of social peer learning. These activities created a morale that kept the pastors involved in theological education.

Some of the readings included authors from historically minoritized groups who represented a variety of different disciplines and experiences: social analysis, the African American context, the social sciences, Catholic and Protestant Hispanic theology, pastoral care, history, liberation theology, urban ministry, Bible, pastoral care, history, urban ministry, spirituality, leadership and management, and case studies. The difficulty was finding readings in Spanish that were from the Latinx US culture. In cases where the language of instruction and reading had to be Spanish, we used materials from Latin America but brought our contextual questions to it.

We used different spaces for a variety of types of theological education: degree programs, supervised ministry, conferences, retreats, and consortia. Theological education includes both informal and formal ways of learning. Its telos is not a grade or a degree but a way of journeying and creating a community that is faithful to the *basileia*. This support system encouraged persons to reach out to and engage experiences and persons they would not have engaged alone.

Community developer and scholar Alexia Salvatierra, reflecting on her experience teaching Latinx pastors in base communities in Los Angeles, explains that pastors are more willing to engage in partnerships in the community with non-Christian organizations and in new practices of community organizing if they meet and engage with their peers who have already done these things.[17] This speaks to the support we all need when shifting perspectives and practices. This is a curriculum that brings together knowledge that is generated from a contextual reality, a dialogical pedagogy, and interdisciplinary information for the doing of theology and a practice of ministry that is relevant mission in our communities.

For the laity, carrying out community service together shapes these practices and the fruits of the Spirit or the virtues that are formed by continuous practice. Laity feel a divide between what we teach and what we practice as congregations. Laity may have deep callings that find no place for expression unless we have congregational practices for carrying out such callings. Practice brings about becoming. Knowing does not come to full fruition without the practices that bring about our becoming into what we preach as communities of faith. The cognitive must be accompanied by the affective, which occurs in our experience of practice and reflection upon the practice. Worship is where we speak of and celebrate the experience of practice and includes our experience of encounter with the Christ. These many places of reflection (the classroom, in the midst of practice, worship) make for the discernment of the values of society in comparison to those of the *basileia*/kingdom. It is this discernment as a community that brings about the wisdom necessary to unmask the idols in our midst and at times expressed in our theology in order to slowly gain the power to practice in accordance with the directions of the *basileia* as a countercultural community.

Curriculum for Generational Tensions

Another area in which theological education is vital is in addressing the tensions between first and second generations in the church about family relationships and leadership in the church. To work on this, the course included both generations in the classroom, even though only the adults were taking the course for credit. Both generations had to read information about immigration history, phases of stabilization, identity formation, stages of psycho-social development, moral development, and Latin@ theology. They had to listen to and analyze each other's music, dramatize for one another a day in their own lives, and role-play. We used fishbowl experiences and exercises from theater of the oppressed to enter into each other's worlds and to switch places with one another.[18] It was very hard work. Each generation had to figure out how to deal with the language barrier. We had a night of theological reflection through poetry, changing the classroom into a café-style setting for spoken-word performances. Participants also had to work collaboratively to create a project for working on generational issues in the church. On the last day, we worked on a mural together that reflected what we had learned and what we wanted our future to look like together. While interpreting the different parts of the mural to each other, everyone began to cry; they had reached a point of mutual appreciation and love for one another. It was an unforgettable moment. It was transformational theological education where the Holy Spirit poured out in our midst.

The discovery was guided by multidisciplinary readings, the surprises to which the arts open us as they catch us off guard, and theological/biblical reflection. The collaborative pieces forced the students to go beyond their comfort zones and to move beyond blame to problem solving. This led to some hard conversations. The aspect of power and authority that ordered the relationship between the two generations had to be guided by the professor by means of rules of engagement for the teaching/

learning process. Eventually this helped to change the patterns of relationship between the generations, and they began to gain a mutual respect for one another based on the giftings they saw in each other rather than traditional cultural roles that are based on authoritarianism or hierarchy. With the new rules for engaging one another, the agency of the younger generation found a space. Here we see how the generational conflicts as a common theme of the curriculum became problem solving as both generations intersected at the place of community and mission. We note how interdisciplinarity and the arts become a part of the curriculum and pedagogy.

Community Development and the Holy Spirit

If the pastors of a community feel powerless to heal the oppression in the community, the tools of community organizing and development would eventually help them to see the power of the Holy Spirit acting in the community, even among and through those partners who at first were suspect, such as nonbelieving leaders of nonprofit multiservice or counseling centers.

"Community development makes sense to the pastors if they can create models that are Holy Spirit centered."[19] This is being done by Salvatierra as she brings pastors together as a part of a certificate program at Fuller Theological Seminary on community development. She has fashioned these cohorts of pastors as cell groups or as base communities, where reflection on the Scriptures in light of the oppressions and traumas of the community takes place by way of community assessment and with the purpose of bringing about healing.

Sustaining this work as part of ministry in the church is difficult, as pastors are typically bivocational and the laity are also engaged in an arduous cycle of survival with two and at times three jobs. This reality prompts us to create pauses in the work that at times disrupt momentum, but we have found they are necessary for people to sustain their commitment long term. In this interim, short retreats for fellowship, reflection, and leisure can serve to sustain perseverance. Also, attention may be placed on the theoretical and theological dimensions of the work, and this can create new foundations upon which to build the next movement of the work. Pastors sit around at such a retreat and joke with one another while also speaking about their lives and ministries with a facilitator who prompts reflection on the work of their ministry as it is connected to their lives. They may bring up problems. The facilitator will foster ways for them to solve problems together and to use the newly learned information and tools in their process.

This is a way of doing theological education that includes the laity as well as the pastors, and that creates spaces for them to learn together and apart. It is a teaching/learning space that is both formal work, part of the traditional system of grades, and informal work, which then is incorporated into the formal learning. Formal and informal learning cross-fertilize each other, incorporating the learning, which is necessary to perspective transformation. The role of the professor is that of a facilitator who integrates the resources of the traditional and nontraditional disciplines of theology, history, pastoral care, and community transformation. Yet, especially with this breadth of resources, it is important that every aspect of the learning be immediately relevant. In addition, the professor must create learning spaces into which the Holy Spirit is welcomed. Such learning spaces include communal discernment exercises, prayer in groups and alone, silence, and listening and sharing together a word from the Lord. It includes formal research that recognizes the presence of the Holy Spirit in ritual and intentional ways, and that integrates the spiritual wisdom that arises.

The Locus of Theological Education

Once again, we can see a communal aspect to theological education here. A group of pastors, theological educators, faith-based community organizers, and lay youth ministers was asked to define theological education. Every person said theological education begins at the places of formation for the Christian life. Thus the life of the community of faith and the learning that takes place in Sunday school, worship, and service are seen as part of theological education. One person even said it begins as the mother sings hymns and praises while the child is still in the womb.[20] In short, the relational aspect is foundational to theological education in the Latinx context. The formational aspects cannot take place without the relational and communal. It is this formational aspect that characterizes the lifelong learning of theological education.

The loci of our theological education are the lakes and oceans of our lives, the intersection of the practical and the theoretical as we move toward pastoral action. Our theology never comes from a blank space.

In such a context, worship is an important part of the teaching/learning ecology. It is where learning is reinforced and incorporated into the memory of the community and its theology. The music becomes a medium of interpretation, integration, and establishment of the new as part of the meaning making of the community and its memory of self. Participation is what reinforces the knowledge. This is knowledge not only as information and application but also as formation. It is knowledge that becomes in us. This becoming in us means that it is knowledge that continues to take new forms of expression in different contexts and it continues to grow and develop rather than merely increase. Increasing can mean that I have more books on shelves or more degrees, but it does not necessarily mean the ability to do effective ministry. Effective ministry includes many dimensions: healing, teaching, social action and justice, networking, conflict management, and fund-raising, among others. It entails the fullness of our being and the practice of our presence and absence. These are things that are not only about what we find in books but also about what we live alongside of others.

Theological education as presently configured cannot integrate all these pieces. We have seen a combination of informal and formal theological education. We have seen the different

spaces in which this takes place, and we have seen the pedagogies that enable social learning and sharing of experiences
from which persons learn in addition to learning from written
research. This is more of a journey than a degree or a curriculum
for ordination. Such learning draws persons to it from a place of
inner thirst and calling, from a desire to become better disciples
and to have the ability to respond adequately to a wound in the
world. One pastor put it this way: "We need to cast our ministry
nets into the waters of anguish." Theological education needs to
be able to go to these deep waters, too.

Wisdom from the Women

At a theological lecture, a group of women challenged me about
the need for spaces for women to do theology together. I told
them that my home would be open to them, as long as they organized themselves. About three months later, they called to let me
know that they were coming. I prepared my home for hospitality
and dialogue, secured it as a women-only space, and anointed it
with prayer for the Holy Spirit to open up the space and to dance
in it. As the women arrived in car pools, they brought out and prepared food, which we placed on the kitchen counter. We prayed
over our feast and sat around the table in the dining room, which
I had enlarged by putting in all its leaves. As we ate together, we
introduced ourselves and our purpose and hopes for being present, specifically our thirst for the Holy Spirit and wholeness, and
our places of relationship, loneliness in ministry, and wound-
edness. We listened intently to one another and poured out the
healing oils of the fullness of our pastoral gifts. It was from this
knowledge of one another and of healing that we began to constitute the space for our theological reflection.

Doing theology together came out of first sharing our lives, in
which we at times reflected on events and subjects of which we
had not spoken publicly before. This meant that insight came to
us in those moments. We recognized this insight and built upon
it. We generated knowledge together as we shared from the dif-

ferent disciplines and varieties of ministry work we were doing. We also wrote. Each time we met, we dedicated thirty to sixty minutes to writing. We passed the writing to another to read what we had written and to give feedback. This too was part of how we generated knowledge together and did theology. We found that our writing was informed not only by our interests but also by our personal life experiences and present *vivencias.*

We always ended our times together by blessing one another around the circle. Each blessing was informed by the things we had heard each other share. As life transitions have moved us to different places, we continue to meet, share, and write together with the help of technology. We continue to invite other women to join us, and the group's diversity enlarges as does its base of knowledge. This is a group with a diversity of generations, Latina cultures, ministry work, and research interests. The fellowship nurtures our deepest theological thoughts and ministry. It is a place of empowerment. Empowerment is connected to author- ity or power given to someone to do something. When people are empowered, they have the self-confidence to carry out their agency or self-determination in their life. To have such power, one must first be aware of oneself as a gifted person in the world and also be aware of who one is in the world. Paulo Freire speaks of critical consciousness, which is first about understanding the world by being able to identify the social, political, historical, economic, and cultural contexts and their contradictions in light of how these influence one's position of power, privilege, or op- pression, and second about using deep reflection with others to strategize and carry out actions that help change these contexts and contradictions by first changing one's own responses to the circumstances.

To come to this critical consciousness, we employed shar- ing about our stories and experiences, listening to each other into spaces of empowerment, and deeply reflecting through writing and feedback. The transformations that took place gave women the freedom to become who they are fully in all the arenas of their lives, including their callings and ministries.

This is a needed spiritual formation part of the curriculum for theological education.

Distance Education

The COVID-19 pandemic has changed education. Schools that had not made a decision about how to use the Internet to educate had to make the decision in a flash to move to virtual spaces for education in order to give continuity to their programs.

Distance education began as early as the 1920s in Latin America, as church leaders were trained via correspondence courses. Evangelism also took place in this way, particularly for hard-to-access communities. Creating community and face-to-face contact in distance learning have taken place through the use of Zoom, BlueJeans, Google hangouts, Skype, and other virtual spaces. Professors have had to educate themselves to teach effectively using these means. Typically, their lectures have become shorter and they use videos and short clips of media content more freely to keep students engaged. If we are intentional about using these media and we balance them pedagogically, they provide ways of engaging multiple intelligences. Discussion boards are ways for students to engage each other in meaningful ways and can prove helpful in making sure that all their voices are heard.

All these media invite educators to rethink their content and more intentionally insert different types of questions along the spectrum of Bloom's taxonomy to develop critical thinking for our students during a semester.[21] Bloom identifies six levels of learning: knowledge, comprehension, application, analysis, synthesis, and evaluation. Knowledge questions test the ability to memorize and recall terms, facts, and details, but such recall does not necessarily equate to comprehension. Comprehension is the capacity to describe or explain in one's own words a new concept that has been introduced. Application encourages students to transfer the knowledge to their own situation or to a context different from their own, while analysis refers to the capacity to break things up into different parts and to figure out the relationship among the parts, finding patterns and inferences. Synthesis questions invite participants to use a combination of ideas from different sources to create something new. Finally, evaluation is for supporting students in their growth in developing opinions and making value decisions about issues based on specific criteria. We work toward these goals in different ways throughout the term, and we develop a variety of exercises to expand the student's capacity to think about the subject matter and to foster learning that lasts.

In virtual education, an action-reflection-action model can guide our resources and modules. The cost, access, training for proper use, maintenance of systems, and technological support require a different level of operations for a school. Capacity building for a long-term vision needs to take place as schools evaluate what they are doing during this transitional time and beyond. Priorities will (and must) change during this transition.

In theological education, field education or teaching for application and for acquiring practical ministerial knowledge offers us both challenges and opportunities at this time. The challenges of social distancing and virtual presence versus embodied presence are very real. In particular, learning to preach and worship via the Internet demands new skills from liturgists and pastors, especially as they retrain those who previously have not had access to or used the Internet in the ways now necessary.

Technology such as Zoom makes it possible to create breakout groups as well as to engage in both synchronous and asynchronous teaching. The types of assignments we plan for students in a time when presence is difficult to negotiate may for now curtail the incarnational nature of pedagogy that we generally are eager to facilitate. Presence is a topic to be reflected upon theologically. Designing experiential learning will depend on how our partnering institutions that are our sites for this learning are conducting their work in the community during this time. Teaching ways of positioning ourselves as the church in the community will necessitate being informed of the changing strategies and learning to read these strategies in light of the mission of the church as light and leaven. The tasks of the church—fellowship, social action, proclamation, teaching social justice, reconceiving economic arrangements, and liturgy—all need to be reevaluated and redefined for our times. The church has come through other times of societal crisis and pandemic. There are several sources of information that are working to keep the church relevant and supplied with what it needs. Denominational Latin@ leaders are providing training, and urban centers for the church are helping leaders to find resources, The Association for Hispanic Theological Education is creating online *conversatorios* (conversations) for doing theological reflection and discussing practice of ministry; local community multiservice centers and other nonprofits in local communities are also sources of help. These are only some of the resource providers. Institutional collaboration is not only a structural issue but also a curricular one, as we seek access to all the resources needed. This is discussed more fully in the next chapter.

The strategy of creative collaboration for mutual challenge and inspiration pushes us to think outside the box and redesign the enterprise of theological education. Other industries have done this by facilitating the exchange of ideas by commingling researchers from different specialties and backgrounds. Communities of practice are one way to do this.

Communities of practice foster learning from experiential realities, dialogue, exchange of information, transference of knowledge, and conversations among those engaged in day-to-day needs and problems. Participants interact, share, and reflect creatively by challenging each other and then building on their best practices. A community of practice functions under the assumption that we learn from our peers and at times generate new sources of knowledge with one another. These communities engage a different set of assumptions about how learning takes place, specifically through the context of our lived experiences as we participate in the world; learning is very much a social phenomenon.

Communities of practice share their practices of theological education at different levels: the administrative, curricular, and theological. These are things that we assume everyone knows and does naturally while not realizing that theological education has been reinvented and re-created. This wisdom or tacit knowledge is hard to communicate in written form. It is an intuitive knowing grounded in our understanding of our values, context, practices, and experiences that have refined our practice. "The concept of practice connotes doing, but not doing in and of itself. It is a doing in a historical and social context that gives structure and meaning to what we do. In this sense, practice is always social practice."[22] This works best if we see theological education as one big ongoing project that belongs to all together and we are connecting to contribute and collaborate on it as a whole. Some members of the Association for Hispanic Theological Education (AETH) engage in this practice in a group they have formed called ReDET—a network of educational entities that I describe more fully in the next chapter. They meet monthly as communities of practice. The knowledge shared is not only quantifiable material in specified disciplines but also rules of thumb, intuitions, embodied understandings, underlying assumptions, and shared worldviews. This is part of tacit knowledge.[23] The diversity of the different ways of thinking and working at a task makes for creative collaboration.

Conclusion

The different pedagogical methods discussed in this chapter all involve reflection in community. As the body of Christ, we know that if one sees a vision, another must help interpret that vision, and a healer, a networker, or a theologian must bring resources to the implementation and rooting in the word of the vision so that all may be edified. Participants collaborate in the creation and increase of knowledge for the improvement of their practice as ministers who benefit the communities their churches serve. The dialogue is at times intergenerational and requires mutual respect. Freirian pedagogy understands this as a process that enhances community, builds social capital, and leads persons to act in ways that make for justice and human flourishing.[24]

The structures that contain this practice are varied. These structures and possibilities for variations on them will be discussed in the next chapter.

4

Las Estructuras Crean Hábitos

A Collaborative Educational Ecology

Every curriculum is framed within an institutional structure. This structure itself is also a part of the curriculum and determines the mission and vision of a school. The people who attend the school, the courses that form the degrees offered, the facilities, the economic arrangements that sustain the school, the faculty and their terms of employment, the forms of delivery for the courses—all these are determined by the structure of the institution. In theological education, traditionally the ecclesial structures that sustain the school also determine the institutional structures.[1] This is the case because theological education has long served the interests of the different church bodies: their mission, ordination requirements, and the knowledge that the church deems necessary for effective ministry. Here I will discuss the structures where the pedagogical practices described above may thrive.

Currently, scholars in the theological disciplines have interests that serve not so much the church but the academy or the disciplines to which they belong. Research and writing (and as a result, teaching) have primarily engaged the questions of the academy rather than the needs of ministry. Some scholars are able to make connections between the academy and the church, while others simply choose to reside within the camp where their interests lie. Some scholars feel that the church limits the scholarly range of discussion. This has created a divide between the interests of the academy and those of the church. The academy sees the church as falling behind the times and as imprisoned within theologies and missions that are no longer relevant to the issues of current society. On the other hand, the church sees the academy as going beyond the orthodoxy of the church or as being incapable of engaging the questions of relevance for the church at a practical and not only a theoretical level. Some churches see scholars as unengaged in the life of the church. Scholars who seek to engage in dialogue in both camps unfortunately become suspect in both.

When I was hired at a theological school considered to be more liberal because professors readily engaged the academy, a pastor visited me and with true concern for me asked what I was doing in "this den of iniquity." Later, at a discussion group at the American Academy of Religion meeting on feminist theologies, a well-meaning colleague told me my scholarly feminist thinking would not advance if I stayed in the church. I understood what led both of these colleagues to their conclusions, but a dialectical dialogue was the ground I was seeking, and I believe that theological education must be a space that hosts this dialectical dialogue. In a global context, to serve only the academy is limiting, as is also to serve only the interests of the church.

How have we come to this bifurcation? In what follows, I briefly examine some of the roots of the model of theological education in which we find ourselves.

Friedrich Schleiermacher and the Fourfold Model

German philosopher and theologian Friedrich Schleiermacher (1768–1834) is credited with fashioning the curriculum for theology at the modern university. His approach was to divide the curriculum into three broad areas: philosophical theology, which focused on Christian theology; historical theology, which looked at the traditions and teachings of the church; and practical theology, which concerned the formation and preparation of church leaders, in particular the clergy. Schleiermacher wanted to bring

Enlightenment arguments into dialogue with the Christian traditions.[2] For him, theology had two functions: one as "a practical discipline for improving general pastoral care in a Christian society," and the other as a "general branch of scholarship" with a capacity to do research and analysis as did the other sciences.[3] This reshaping of theology at the University of Berlin, where Schleiermacher was a professor, combined with legacies of English and Scottish universities to shape the dominant model of theological education in the United States. Over time, the US model settled into four areas: biblical studies, dogmatics/systematic theology, historical studies/history of Christianity, and practical or pastoral studies. The original intent was for all four to be tied together in ways that contributed to the improvement of pastoral leadership. The paradigm developed a life of its own in theological education in the United States.

Scholar Edwin Aponte questions whether this model from the nineteenth century is relevant to the needs of communities of color and posits that "the fourfold curriculum devalues practice and is not friendly to diverse communities of learning across racial, ethnic, gender, sexuality, and class boundaries"—and that it actually never did consider the varied contexts of persons of different cultures who were living in oppressive dominant culture contexts.[4] As such, the philosophical systems of thought that formed this paradigm assumed racist perspectives of the world.[5] This affects not only the ideological dimensions of theological education but also the institutional dimensions. Within this system, Latinx students have reported experiencing race and class discrimination and oppression.[6] Latinx faculty often do not find it a hospitable environment. The nature of their academic projects tends to be more collaborative and multiperspectival and interdisciplinary, which, in a system with individualistic values, is neither honored nor considered sufficiently scholarly or of necessary quality. Pedagogical approaches also follow this understanding of individualism, and curricula too often fail to include multiple perspectives. Non-European faculty and students experience this as oppression. Aponte calls for seminaries to engage in critical and constructive ways the changes needed in ideologies and "pedagogies of oppression, in the hope of justice and reconciliation."[7] These changes would reflect structures that facilitate more collaborative ways to engage in problem solving and contextual theological reflection along with other disciplines so as to respond to the globalization of the twenty-first century. Scholarship is informed by asking: What is the purpose of one's research and teaching within the particular broad context in which one is living?

The identification and discussion of these issues are not new, for already in 1997 Catholic theologian Gary Riebe-Estrella suggested that in order to hold in tension the two movements reenvisioning the doing of theology and reenvisioning of the tradition, theological education needed to be more than information banking. Instead, he argued, it needed to be a sustained conversation in which students would focus on issues of praxis and the tradition and how these mutually engage and challenge each other. For this conversation to take place, Riebe-Estrella insisted that theological education needs to be interdisciplinary.[8] This call for interdisciplinarity challenges the fourfold structure that dominates faculty appointment, retention, and promotion in seminaries and Bible institutes.

Education in the Age of Information

In a time when commodification and exploitation have invaded all realms of life—family, health, education, friendships, celebrations, and symbols—and have thus influenced the logic of life, the purpose of theological teaching becomes that of social justice. This goal invites us to consider the discussion about theological education on a global scale.

Each time the economy and the sciences change, so do business and education. In the midseventies a shift began to take place from an industrial society to the information age. This shift has changed the workforce and the way we educate persons for the workforce.

The information age no longer requires a massive workforce that includes assembly line workers, foremen, supervisors, and data processors. Instead it requires so-called mind workers such as teachers, engineers, scientists, executives, and attorneys. On the other side of the employment spectrum, it calls for low-wage service workers who usually do not receive benefits (like health insurance) for their work. These service workers' jobs are increasingly outsourced to developing countries where wages are even lower. The level of education necessary for a well-paying and satisfying job has changed However, even with college education, today's jobs require that persons come into the workforce with the skills for problem solving and the ability to learn how to learn. Furthermore, during their lifetime, workers will need to engage in ongoing education in order to keep up with the fast-paced changes in technology. They must be able to work creatively and collaboratively, and to apply the knowledge of their degree.

Besides all that, "the venue for education is also changing from public schools to multiple venues such as homes, church buildings, learning centers, anywhere that one can put a computer and have access to the web. The uniform system of educating is changing to a custom designed system in accordance [with] the students' needs and interests."[9] Critical thinking and scientific inquiry are necessary to nurture the ability to solve complicated problems, find the information required, and apply skills and information to problem solving. Library facilities and actual physical texts are now only one among many forms of storing and accessing information. In our technological age, information is digital. Videos, websites, podcasts, social media, and databases give access to information. Collaborative educational projects necessitate that all these forms be accessible. This has implications for the structure of a school. More schools than ever before are seeking to work with each other, and they typically use technology for such collaboration.

Because education has been the way to mainstream persons into society, it is important that we note the fuller context of theological education within the broader spectrum of education as well as the issue of equity in education. The issue of access to education is connected to the economic means of a community. Allan Collins and Richard Halverson point out that "schools have been the means by which many immigrants and minorities gained access to the mainstream and are therefore the institutions that foster equity more than any other institution."[10] This speaks to the need for church leaders in immigrant or poor communities to have access to and knowledge of how educational systems work, as they will be sought out for information. Leaders also have the unique opportunity to make their congregations or church structures a contributing part of the educational ecology or configuration.

A configuration is an alignment of elements in a particular form that allows for the contribution of greater fullness of things. An educational configuration could take various elements that provide information, socialization, and skill that allow persons to adapt to and survive in society. Another configuration could bring together the family and the church to show how, together, we teach values and a lifestyle that show that we value persons. We believe in the worth of all persons because they are created in the image of God. We could add to this configuration schools or social media, a sports program or a museum's science exhibits and programs. All these elements become sources of information and contribute to greater dimensions of the development of persons. The potential is clearly present. The question is: How is a Bible institute part of the educational configurations in a community?

Theological education in the Latinx context holds possibilities for creating avenues of access to the different levels of education in ways that can transcend language and other barriers. A Bible institute may be the first educational institution to which a person has access in the United States. If the Bible institute is connected to other institutions of learning, such as a Bible college or seminary, it becomes an incentive for someone to move forward, and a point of entry into the larger educational spectrum of higher education. In light of this broader scenario of education in an age of information, for the Latin@ church, theological education falls within the fuller spectrum of educational access starting in kindergarten and continuing through "grade" sixteen. It is a much larger issue than just the education of the pastor, as it entails the education of the entire Latin@ community in which the church, and therefore the pastor and other lay leaders, needs to find ways to address these issues in the neighborhoods where it ministers. In a knowledge-based economy, education is a fundamental requirement for the economic success of any group. For the church, access to education is an important aspect of addressing social justice for the Latinx community. This falls within the understanding of *misión integral.*

When a church becomes involved in the educational ecology of a community, its leaders may become role models and the church may perform a variety of functions. One of these is to act as a cultural broker between school staff, administration, and the community—including the small businesses in the community. Such a relationship may in turn benefit the school, hospitals, banks, and other entities that provide some form of education to the community as one of their products and services. The theological education of immigrant pastors serves as a socializing agent that reorients the vision and mission of ministry to include this type of role for the church as an expression of a larger vision of social justice. When pastors are not theologically educated, or when their education stays within the confines of the traditional understanding of the role of the church as a mainly religious institution that brings only a message of personal and not societal transformation as well, the community transformation dimension of their mission is left out. Nonetheless, pastors and their congregants all have the same needs in their communities. Soon they recognize that something more than prayer is needed in order to thrive. The second generation, those born in the United States to immigrant parents, will form a faith that needs this dimension of transformation. If the church is not flexible enough in its theology and mission to form this sort of faith, this generation will seek other places of worship—if they stay with the Christian faith at all.

For Latin@s in the mainline churches, the current dominant definitions of the church do not fit the realities of the communities they serve. Neither does the theological education that those churches provide. The models of education of those who belong to church councils that are Latin@-run have been defined by the dominant-culture evangelical church bodies that evangelized them. The theological view upon which these educational models are based promotes the idea that there is one "truth" that must be adhered to, and the curriculum is based on the knowledge of this "truth." The mission of such churches is to evangelize, and evangelization is defined almost exclusively as concerning the soul of the person, with little attention to the roots of the economic or political realities where the person lives. Theological education is therefore constructed using the same curricular structure of categories as the mainline or evangelical dominant structures and theologies. These follow Schleiermacher's fourfold model.

Theological Education and the Function of the Latin@ Church in the Diaspora

Rather than do a full critique of the structure of theological education and how curriculum determines that structure, my purpose is once again to speak of possibilities or alternatives. Such alternatives can act as catalysts for readers' conversations with others on the present structures, with a view to how the gospel needs to serve the present generation in a context influenced by globalization. Because of globalization, it is important to speak in broad strokes of the larger function of the church for Latin@s in the diaspora, and of how theological education enhances or disempowers the Latin@ church.

In a study entitled "The Theological Education of U.S. Hispanics," sociologist Edwin I. Hernandez and others maintain that the church stands at the center of the Latin@ community.[11] Churches, they say, "maintain meaning, communicate values, sustain cultural identity, and organize for empowerment and justice."[12] As such, faith communities contribute to the health and well-being of the Latinx community in which they find themselves by providing counseling; social services advocacy; community outreach; services to children, youth, and seniors; shelter, food, and clothing; immigration legal services and advocacy; job training; and so forth.[13] However, the strength of the church is dependent on the experiences and education of its leadership. For this reason, the theological education of church leadership is crucial to the development not only of the church but also of the community churches serve. What elements of theological education are necessary for fortifying this ecology of strength and vitality in the Latinx community? Are the current model and curricula of theological education meeting the needs of this leadership? Where does the Latinx pastoral and lay leadership receive training that addresses these needs? To answer these questions, we return for a moment to the global context, and then discuss possible structures of collaboration.

Implications of Globalization for Interdisciplinary Structure of Theological Education

In the third decade of the twenty-first century, the world faces a global paradigm shift. In this context, a new concept emerges: the "creation of shared value." Coined by Harvard professors Michael Porter and Mark Kramer, the term refers to the renewal of capitalism based on the symbiosis between business interests and the needs and challenges facing modern civilization. "Companies must reconnect business success with social progress." According to this theory, the great wave of innovation and wealth that will allow the growth of the world economy will be generated through shared value.[14] Shared value "advances the competitiveness of a company while simultaneously advancing the economic and social conditions in the communities it operates in. . . . It expands the connections between societal and economic progress."[15]

Now, more than ever, it is necessary to develop an innovative culture and link it with a sustainable economy in order to meet the social and environmental challenges facing the world. Inviting economists and theologians to be in dialogue with one another and with a group of pastors would benefit a community. The dialogue would be imbued with the values of the *basileia*. Notice how this requires multiple perspectives. The scholars and professors who engage in such dialogues must see their work as collaborative if they are to be in the service of a global society.

This type of integration and dialogue between disciplines is what the new generation is seeking. Millennials and Generation Z will be the most educated generations the Latinx community has ever had. As they learn to love God as newly formed professionals, they are no longer looking at the American dream as their goal in the way their grandparents perhaps did. Instead, they stress the importance of social justice goals. This means they are asking questions about social ethics and Christian values as these connect to the work of their vocations in a global context. Here is where a discussion about shared value becomes important. Some of the new generation are coming to theological education because they are social entrepreneurs who approach "business and societal issues from a value perspective, which business has treated as peripheral matters."[16] This generation wishes to be educated for a call or Christian vocation in the arenas that their parents were perhaps not able to enter, and they have enough faith and belief that Christ is indeed Lord of all to trust that those arenas can be transformed. Theological education in dialogue with other disciplines helps them to acquire the skills necessary to practice social justice and the theological thinking necessary to articulate what they are doing in their professions within the framework of the Christian tradition. In this way, they expand and deepen the Christian tradition for a new global society.

A generation with these hopes needs theological education that goes beyond the fourfold breakdown of disciplines. It needs theological education that ensures that seminaries that stand independent of the other disciplines find ways to collaborate with the larger educational ecology in their midst if their vision and theology are to be holistic. Theological education in a global society calls us to take fully into account the varied cultural patterns and differences, with worldviews, language ecologies, assessment diversification, standards for learning, and rules of discourse that engage everyone at the table and beyond. These negotiations require that we think about how to open paths of conversation and collaboration between universities and seminaries. Teachers, administrators, learners, and church and community leaders now have new roles. They are responsible for considering what is to be taught to whom, who should teach it, and for what purposes. Religion serves as a language of values for this discourse.

Addressing Diversities of Theological Thinking

Charles Foster has some helpful insights for thinking about diversity in terms of the pattern of values that sustains diversity. To include diversities of thinking entails learning assessments that are as diverse as our students. It also means diversifying assignments we give to prompt critical thinking, as well as the ways in which different learners do critical thinking.[17] Important distinctions in developmental patterns and ways of knowing show different ways of understanding the role of thinking. For some persons, this means thinking in order to know the truth so that one may be obedient to that truth, and "to discern with increasing clarity what the faith tradition has identified as concrete and objective truth."[18] In other learning contexts, critical thinking is for imagining beyond the limits of the tradition. Such thinking "leads to the 'wide-awakeness' that Maxine Greene describes as the quest of teachers to demystify taken-for-granted assumptions and perspectives that blind us to the limits of our truth claims."[19] Lastly, some seek the truth as known by one's own community. This Foster calls contextual truth—"a truth large enough to encompass diverse cultural and ecclesial perspectives on Christian tradition."[20] To be inclusive of these types of thinking, one must keep a pedagogical structure that secures a dialogical interaction between pedagogies of formation and pedagogies of empowerment.[21]

In fairness to teachers, a teaching/learning structure that wishes to sustain this type of diversity of thinking across its curriculum requires ongoing teacher training and sharing of successful strategies and problem solving among teachers. Teachers may form into communities of practice that facilitate reflection on practice and collaboration to share resources for such pedagogical practices. A community of practice is a group of persons who participate in the same craft or profession and who come together to share innovations, solve problems, and learn new practices.[22]

It is clear that the diversity of thinking about truth and critical thinking originates among the diverse ecclesial bodies and their theological expressions. A theological teaching institution maintains a relationship with the different ecclesial bodies of its students by including their representatives on its board of directors or trustees. This ensures that the same type of thinking about what it means to learn and to teach in these ways is taking place at the institutional board level.

Independent seminaries and, at times, even those embedded within a denominational university have an enclosed structure that makes it more complicated to communicate across curricular disciplines, making interdisciplinary dialogue more difficult. The day-to-day operations and committee commitments of faculty take up so much time that it is easier to stay within the familiar. Yet precisely in such a situation people need structures that foster ongoing interdisciplinary exchange. A once-a-month meeting with a different department, whether at the same school or at a different school, could become a practice for faculty. These new practices need to be incentivized by including them in tenure or contractual structures.

As institutions increasingly cut back on full-time faculty, this type of intentional, systematic conversation becomes difficult to sustain because of the time and space required. It thus becomes helpful to form teaching/learning collaboratives in which institutions covenant together to sustain each other in common goals of teaching and learning in theological education. A collaboration among different theological entities can create partnerships and projects to sustain common needs, such as digital library resources, teacher training, reflection on technology, and the sharing of professors.

Collaborative Models of Theological Education

One organization that facilitates such a structure of collaboration is the Association for Hispanic Theological Education (AETH). AETH is a network of Bible institutes, seminaries, and other theological entities that provides accessible and affordable theological training for pastors and lay leaders across the United States and Puerto Rico. The network includes community experts and leaders, educators, researchers, directors of educational institutions, pastors, denominational leaders, NGO (nongovernmental organization) leaders and FBOs (faith-based organizations), authors, lecturers, and students. Taking 150 as the average number of students per institution, one can estimate 51,300 students in the 342 Bible institutes in AETH's database; this is almost twelve times more than the number of Hispanic students in all seminary programs as reported by Association for Theological Schools (ATS) in 2017 (4,460).[23]

"AETH's mission is its commitment to respond to this need for the Hispanic church to be led by pastors and leaders with the appropriate theological training to minister effectively, leading their members in their service to the community and society at large."[24] This ministry is to be carried out in communities that face the challenges of poverty and low educational attainment, violence, and discrimination. The multigenerational challenges of an immigrant community are also present with language issues that divide the generations. Denominational bodies oftentimes have scant resources to help meet these challenges or to provide for the training of leaders to meet them. Most pastors are bi- or tri-vocational, so finding the time and resources for expensive theological education is not an option. Furthermore, if the theological education offered is not relevant to these needs, then potential students quickly realize it is not a wise way to spend their time and money.

Bible institutes are designed to bring together the practical and the theoretical so that practical and daily aspects of pastoral work are discussed in relevant ways. Finding the resources and skills to meet the aforementioned needs in contextual ways can be a challenge for Bible institutes, especially those directed by bi- and tri-vocational personnel and professors. This is where AETH comes in. It is creating a network of Bible institutes that covenant to collaborate on common needs and projects and share resources with one another. These institutions are spread across the United States and Puerto Rico, and some of them work with students in Latin America. To facilitate their collaboration, they have begun to be formed as communities of practice by people who "share a concern or a passion for something they do and [who] learn how to do it better as they interact with one another regularly."[25] These communities of practice engage in social learning.

Given the nature of the tri-vocational leadership, most Bible institutes have worked in isolation from one another. Yet more recently, a growing number of institutes with membership in AETH have become increasingly willing to work collaboratively. This is a culture shift that AETH has sought to nurture by opening channels of cooperation and communication between them; fostering spiritual, professional, and institutional development among its members; and working toward greater enrollment of Hispanics in their institutes called ReDET (*Red para Entidades Teologicas*, "the network of theological entities"). Importantly, ReDET allows members to focus on concerns and issues unique to their respective regions, and to create venues for development and enhancement of leadership skills and relationship building in their particular geographic areas. It also supports increased networking, sharing of ideas, best practices, and peer learning. It is the collective learning process that bonds them. This collective learning is an experience in itself, as communities of practice reflect upon their learning and upon varied ways of putting that learning into practice. The interactions also "produce resources that affect their practice whether or not they engage in the actual practice of it together."[26]

Such professional learning makes it easier to generate knowledge from one's praxis. It benefits the institution through conversations in which solutions to problems, assessment of these solutions, innovations, tips and tricks, and best practices are shared. In this way, the organization as a whole, and not just the faculty or administration, benefits from the continuous flow of ideas and knowledge. Research on communities of practice suggests that even if contact is done virtually (or through a combination of in-person and virtual contact), through extended relationships with one another and by sharing stories and experiences, the group can form a collective identity and can continue to grow, including through enculturation for practitioners who are novices. For this to take place, all members of the community of practice must participate. An able facilitator of this contributing dynamic is necessary. The facilitator keeps a record of the ideas, resources, and the discourse. Facilitators are the keepers of the knowledge that is being generated and lift it before the group for their continued reflection and evaluation.[27]

This collaboration can create a different type of institution for theological education. For example, many different institutes may share one library virtually by connecting with one partner seminary or school. They may exchange professors, thus guaranteeing that all professors that teach at their institution have degrees, and in this way bring their Bible institute to the level of bachelor equivalency, making it possible for students to go on to master's-level work at a different school. The professors, who are typically pastor-scholars, are sustained primarily by one institution (a university, college, or seminary) or by bivocational work while sharing their teaching work to provide quality instruction for a Bible institute. The teaching is counted as part of their teaching load, since it creates a relationship with students who (it is expected) later become a part of the university, college, or seminary.

This type of exchange creates a situation whereby the pay of the professor is shared by the different institutions and it makes theological education affordable for students; it also cross-fertilizes the research of a scholar or becomes a work of justice of a school. The "win" for the school is that it becomes a feeder of master's program candidates. The flexibility of the exchange makes it possible to include its interdisciplinary dimensions and to include other community leaders as a part of it. This flexible model of collaboration also allows seminary or college students to take a course at a Bible institute and gain from the more practical dialogue of that classroom with a student body that has experience in pastoring. A memorandum of understanding (MOU) could sustain the exchange negotiations.

An example of this type of collaboration is Western Theological Seminary in Holland, Michigan, which is forming an MOU with a Bible institute called Educando Creyentes Hacemos Ministros (ECHAM) in Puerto Rico; in this exchange the instructors of ECHAM are able to work toward their master's degrees at Western through online classes. Attempts are being made to establish affordable costs for the students. Another example: McCormick Theological Seminary has an agreement with the Apostolic Assembly to educate their bishops and key leaders through their Spanish masters course. The Apostolic Assembly is one of the fastest-growing Hispanic Pentecostal denominations in the United States, with over seven hundred churches nationwide; it has more than four hundred churches in twenty countries.[28]

Collaboration could also include sharing other technological resources. This could include electronic library databases, which are quite expensive but which collaboration could make affordable for all.

Such larger communities of practice are only one way institutions might avail themselves of collaborative, ongoing learning amidst great change taking place in higher education today. Other Latin@ institutions or churches partner with churches in Africa or Latin America that they have helped to birth or that are connected to their denomination or other type of ecclesial body to provide online theological education. While some of these programs are totally online, others offer a hybrid of online and in-person learning: students come to the United States or a regional location for an intensive course and then do the rest of their work online. Some of these programs have teachers or helping pastors on the ground who establish fellowship among the students, and tutoring or peer learning may take place at that location. Online access may be provided at one central regional location for anyone who does not have it.

Creating Educational Ecologies

Let's look at how Bible institutes could initiate collaboration to create or expand an ecology of education in their community. To do this, I will sketch how an ecological system works and compare this with an educational ecology. In an ecological environment, there are living organisms such as birds, plants, and worms, and nonliving elements such as the wind, the soil, and the sun. Among the organisms are producers of energy and consumers of energy. The interaction between these, the ways in which they create a habitat, determines which species will survive in an environment. A Bible institute (BI) can be a producer of energy and thus help create a more life-giving habitat—but not if it exists in isolation. It must interact in collaborative ways with similar entities.

A BI has the possibility of cultivating bilingual/bicultural engagement. It can create ways to leverage a variety of forms of education, both formal and informal. It can also provide education for persons to adapt and to survive in the environment. If we connect the BI to another educational entity that provides general education, then BI students can gain access to an undergraduate degree. If the BI connects to a seminary, the students can gain access to graduate religious studies or theological education.

But let's go beyond the traditional forms of education. A BI might provide classes in English or Spanish as a second language, both for workers in the community who serve dominant Spanish speakers and for members of its second and third generations who wish to reconnect to their language roots. Given the health needs of the communities they serve, BIs might provide health education by making the connection to the value of our body as the temple of the Holy Spirit. Likewise, BIs are in an excellent position to share information with the community about knowing our rights as immigrant persons, or about financial literacy.

In a technological age, education is a must, and we still have persons in our community without so much as a high school diploma. Thinking creatively to address this lack, I wonder: Might a Bible institute offer GED classes? In addition to serving the church community, a BI could also be a community educational center that houses other educational partners as well. Such a synergy of symbiotic relations can give expression to a larger witness of the *basileia*.

But there is more: Our Latinx community has a very young population. Many of us are in our childbearing years, and children five years old and younger are the biggest single age group among us. How about offering parenting classes? Latin@s are also great consumers in the United States, but our money typically does not stay in our communities. Spending by the Latinx community has increased more than spending in non-Latinx households. *Hispanics: Demographic and Consumer Spending Trends* reports that "Hispanic consumers have become the most important driver of growth in a wide variety of consumer expenditure categories."[29] This calls for fostering entrepreneurial and financial literacy skills. It is also important to have discussions about consumerism and the values of the *basileia*. Theological education that is guided by a vision of *misión integral* will reach to every sphere of life.

CHAPTER 4

A Biblical Parallel

Consider this: During the Babylonian exile, the Israelites did not
have access to the temple and therefore could no longer practice
the rituals of their worship (such as their sacrifices). Priests were
not needed. It was probably during this time that the synagogue
emerged as an institution. Ever after, the synagogue has been
a center for maintaining religious and cultural identity. Today,
immigrant churches likewise seek to maintain religious and
cultural identity after being taken away from traditional institutions. The BI, working in tandem with others in the educational
ecology, could be where such identity formation takes place in
the community, along with homes.

In ecology, an organism capable of synthesizing its own food
from inorganic substances using light is known as an autotro-
phic organism. Green plants are such organisms. In the Bible,
the righteous are compared to trees that yield fruit in season.
Both the righteous and trees receive the light necessary to flour-
ish from Jesus, the Light. The good tree is nurtured by the waters of life. In like manner, autotrophs in the ecosystem are
interdependent. And so too BIs cannot produce everything by
themselves. They need to collaborate; they need to work with
someone to produce or create something. In this case the collaboration is in order to generate life and hope. And they need
Jesus shining down on them. Jesus is our light and living water,
and we create an institution—the Bible institute—as a vessel that
gives life in our communities. In ordinary language this is called
social impact.

Through certification, AETH has enabled BIs to have greater
impact and value as collaborating partners in the ecology of
education in partnership with the Association for Theological
Schools (ATS). Certification provides "institutional and educational standards for Bible institutes with two goals in mind: (a) to
promote and improve the theological education of eligible Bible institutes so that their graduates function at a baccalaureate
level and are equipped to become leaders for the radical trans-

formation of church and society, and (b) to provide accessible pathways to enrollment in ATS-accredited graduate theological schools for graduates of AETH-certified Bible institutes."[30] The standards align with the minimal educational and institutional standards that are equivalent to baccalaureate-level studies. The process helps to make the BIs and partnering institutions interdependent. The Center for Hispanic Theological Education in California (CHET) works interdependently with the Evangelical Covenant Church beyond its Latin@ membership. They are connected to many different ecclesiastical bodies, and they have built a board that represents and sustains this strength. The Seminario Pentecostal works interdependently with the Pentecostal Theological Seminary of the Church of God in Cleveland, Tennessee. The Latin@ bishops of the Church of God sustain this relationship and are able to build capacity for their BIs by nurturing the development of their own professors, who in turn reflect theologically and produce Latin@ Pentecostal theology for a *pastoral*, or pastoral action. *Pastoral* is a Spanish word that encompasses the tending of the souls of the people, the preaching and discipleship, as well as the church's response to the needs of the community mission. It is the whole of the congregation's actions of spiritual and prophetic care and formation informed by its continuous theological reflection. The students of the Seminario Pentecostal, which has been certified by AETH, transition into the Pentecostal Theological Seminary, thus increasing the number of MDiv enrollees.

This same interdependence can take place among several BIs in the same region or across the United States and Puerto Rico. There can be a synergy that allows all to share the particularity of the gifts that each one has as an institution. In 2 Corinthians, Paul writes about coming to Corinth to collect an offering for those in Jerusalem who are in need. He prepares the Corinthians' giving spirit by saying: "It is not our intention that others may be relieved while you are burdened, but that there may be equality. *At the present time, your surplus will meet their need, so that in turn their surplus will meet your need. Then there will be equality. As it is written: 'He who gathered much had no excess, and he who gathered little had no shortfall'"* (2 Cor. 8:13–15, Berean Study Bible). This passage understands equality as sufficiency for all. Paul is creating an interdependence between the congregations in different places. Interdependence is the quality or condition of being mutually reliant on each other. In some respects each of us has plenty, but in other respects we need something from others.

In much the same way, AETH has worked with the independent structures of its members. It has created some things for the benefit of all, such as books for Bible institutes and seminarians authored by Latinx scholars, which makes them more relevant for teaching and more representative of the voices of the collective Latinx wisdom and *pastoral*. Because of AETH's leadership and strength of sharing through its networks, and in partnership with the Hispanic Theological Initiative that nurtures Latinx scholars and the Hispanic Summer Program where Latinx scholars offer courses that express Hispanic/Latinx theology relevant to Latin@ ministries, some BIs have done a considerable amount of capacity building and now have the potential to become a resource to others. As a result, the number of Latinx scholars has increased.

Imagining the Future

We have looked at how Bible institutes, working as a part of a collaborative educational ecology, can connect with other theological entities to provide theological education and can build capacity so that resources for learning can be shared across the board. We have seen how a BI can become a center of learning in the community that, for example, can offer health education for diabetes, prenatal care and nutrition, and regular health clinics, and can teach Spanish or English as a second language. Thanks to this structure of collaboration, vocation, and *basileia*, values may be integrated for Latinx professional generations who hunger for discussions about ethical issues and decision making, for example.

Imagine Bible institutes that become a part of these inter-disciplinary discussions. How would our theology, our worship, our preaching be transformed? How would our neighborhood institutions be changed if we, the church, could bring our contributions to the table to share? Imagine a discussion that seeks to create a *pastoral* for immigration or citizenship alongside other professionals who are seeking just solutions for this dilemma. How would these discussions be expanded, and how would *la pastoral* be transformed if we sat together at the same table to reconsider these issues?

For our younger generations, we could create curricula that form radical disciples of Jesus by including spiritual practices, simple living, and social justice practices for creating an order of prophets. In a community with limited resources for providing private music, art, sports, and exercise classes, making BIs into collaborative community centers could help make these activities available and affordable. Imagine BIs connected to Christian colleges for providing associate in arts and bachelor of arts degrees or for offering GED programs and financial literacy that would make possible financial planning for education.

As a social institution, higher education has enacted this function through its activities related to preparing and educating students; it has also been a crucible for social transformation. During contentious battles in the nation about who should be entitled to benefit from living in a "land of opportunity," higher education has been a major catalyst for enacting pathways to full citizenship and participation. The structures of each institution need to be designed specifically to create pathways of collaboration and a flow of degree and course work between institutions so that these ecologies could be of financial benefit to all as well.

Financial replacement value refers to how much it would cost others to provide the same services or programs with similar resources. At how much do you think we could assess the annual replacement value of the work of a Bible institute operating as an ecology of educational collaboration? More than social capital, this structural partnership is a glimpse of the *basileia*. Thy kingdom come, thy will be done, oh Lord, through the collaborative efforts of theological education! Let us work together so that our surplus will meet another's need, so that in turn the other's surplus will meet our need. "Then there will be equality" (2 Cor. 8:14).

These are only the signs of the new things of which we will speak in the following chapter.

5

Cosas Nuevas

Considerations for Conversations and Innovations

Many times I have been inspired by the preaching of the Isaiah passages that speak of the new things that God is doing and will do. Though we perk up in our pews to hear about new things coming, that same enthusiasm often dissipates when it comes time to actually make room for the new or when we understand what birthing the new entails. What happens to the old when the new comes? Though we might complain about it, the old is at least familiar. We have established ourselves upon it. New things in a community of faith come with different ways of making meaning of our faith or of what the Scriptures are saying to us. The tradition has become the filter through which we read the Scriptures. When the Spirit breathes new life into the interpretation of the text, we are not always ready to hear what it says to us. If it doesn't sound familiar, we are quick to believe that it is unorthodox or not *sana doctrina* (sound doctrine). But discernment beckons us to listen and sit with the unfamiliar, to critique it against the larger record of the text.

This is what the Christians did during the first council of the church. Acts 15 shows us that they listened carefully to the wit-

---

In this chapter I make use of portions of my previous writings: "Doing Theology," *Journal of Common Ground* 1, no. 2 (Spring 2004): 2–10 and *Hispanic Bible Institutes: A Community of Theological Construction* (Scranton, PA: Scranton University Press, 2004).

ness of the Spirit, who was doing new things among the gentiles, even baptizing the new gentile believers in the Spirit before they were baptized in water or circumcised. After listening to the witness of these new things from Paul and Peter, those gathered waited on the Spirit in silence. James brought forth a Scripture that had not been used before to understand these matters of circumcision. The Scripture came to them in a new way and brought resolution to the seeming incongruence of the new things of the Spirit and the familiar things of the tradition. This process of communal discernment reactualized the tradition. Further reading of the letters of Paul shows us that the matter was not completely resolved by the time the letters of the apostles were received into the canon, but that some groups continued to hold on to the previous understandings of the tradition. For them and for us, it is difficult to live into the new.

The trauma of immigration, of having to leave our country of origin and come to a new nation, especially when that new nation does not receive us hospitably, rips us from that which is familiar. In such circumstances, the faith community is often the place where we reestablish the familiar and the feeling of being welcome. This makes it even more difficult to hear of new things in the Spirit. Yet our children and our children's children, those who have not had the things of our countries of origin ingrained into them firsthand, have to find ways to plant vineyards and build houses and marry in the new land (Jer. 29), and they need the tradition to speak to new life situations in order to be guided forward. Discrimination, poverty, the racism narrative and more recent attacks of white supremacists, the lure of wealth—all these require that the next generations create values to guide them in the faithful practice of their faith, that they do critical thinking, and that their faith also be critiqued in order to be strengthened for navigating these new passageways. The faith must speak to these new matters; it must give the community ways to understand and to conduct themselves so that they are under the covering of righteousness and not victims of such oppressions.

Those of us who remain in our countries of origin need to critique our life situations and especially the political corruptions that affect our socioeconomic realities so that we can respond to them in ways that incarnate the message of the gospel of righteousness and so that our lands can be healed. These are the types of situations that nudge us to reactivate and refresh the tradition.

For those of us whose journey has been immigration, the new is an interruption or disruption in the familiar that has sustained us for as long as we can remember. The number of persons leaving the church because it does not help them find and create meaningful and purposeful lives speaks to how the familiar has become the irrelevant. For such persons in particular, we must pray for the winds of the Spirit to bring new life.

For such complex matters, we need not only the usual tools of theology and Bible but also the tools of sociology, psychology, economics, ecology, and medicine to analyze the situation responsibly and to be able to give an incarnated, wise public witness of our faith in the public square, where persons wonder where God is. It is in the public square that we might already find the new things of God taking place. And it is the church that needs to seek after the Lord, who is found in spaces the church sometimes does not imagine itself to be. This is part of mission as well.

How do we make way for the new things of the Spirit in such a situation? For whether we have listened or not, over the centuries it has been the Spirit who has heard our cries for freedom from oppression, from violence, from the plunder of our lands, from the lies that have persuaded us to see ourselves through the eyes of the colonizer and to participate in making ourselves into the image that the colonizers and not God have ordained for us. We have colluded so long in our own subjugation and voicelessness that we wonder whether the narrative of the Word of God can truly provide a discourse of worthiness and a voice for us. Or has interpretation of the Word been obscured and misshapen by colonized understandings of who we are and what our place is in society? Has the interpretation of God's Word been stymied by the religious rather than being enlivened by the Spirit? How can we tell the difference? How does the study of the Bible and theology at our Bible institutes address this? How does our pastoral work speak to it? When we study church history, do we recognize this trajectory of the Word and of the church? Do we make our students aware of it and ask critical questions so as to empower our students to create a *new* story of faithfulness?

Reviving the Reformation

If the language of colonizer and oppressor seems strange and bothersome to you in light of theological education, ask yourself *why*. Where did we get the notion and understanding that these concepts and issues are not a part of the church? Why do we think they are coming from someone who is confusing the sacred with the secular or is full of too much wine from the academic world? Why have we separated these issues of oppression from worship and mission? How is it that we respond to these by way of the parousia, believing that the church should be only about worshiping Jesus, who will come one day and sweep us away from these afflictions? Don't we, right now, work in the world and make decisions about how it will function? Don't we buy and sell in this world and have need of employment and food, shelter and clothing? Didn't Jesus come to this world and engage it and denounce those among his people who colluded with the Romans and their systems of oppression? We also participate in and maintain these systems. We complain about them and speak of how they need to change. We seek to defend our children from the systems that would do them harm and that keep them from the dreams we have for them and the dreams they have for themselves. Why is the church not speaking about this, and why is it not a part of her mission? Why is prayer our only response about such pervasive daily concerns? And how do we expect such prayer to be answered? Why don't we do something? Does God simply help us to bear such systemic afflictions? Does God magically make something happen? Or does God perhaps call the church to be a part of God's work in the world in relationship to these matters? Who told us that these matters are not a concern of God and the work of the church?

The theological significance of this language becomes clearer when we remember the Reformation as a comprehensive social movement, a mission to reform every part of life. In those days of clergy dominance and abuses of clergy power, the declaration of *sola fide*—that faith alone saves us—stripped the church (or rather, its clergy) of one kind of authority, an authority that led people to depend on actions and payments to save their souls. Could a new spirit of Reformation strip us of the fears left by the evangelizing legacy that was infused by colonialism where we learned to pray but not to march, for example? *Sola fide* provided the opportunity, for the first time, to dare to interpret the salvific revelation in broader terms and not only from the spiritual or merely personal. A parallel confession of the Reformation, *sola Scriptura*, insisted that Scripture alone offers a definitive revelation of the God we know in Jesus Christ. Believers can therefore call upon Scripture to challenge traditions in and beyond the church.

These confessions of *sola fide* and *sola Scriptura* were not just abstract academic assertions. They brought to people freedom of conscience and a sense of agency, both individual and collective. The organization of society took a different turn with regard to authority at all levels: the political, the economic, and the religious. Through the Reformation, a doctrinal dispute became a social movement.

The social movement unleashed by the Reformation did not just revise doctrines in theology books. The changes in doctrinal understanding opened the doors to an energy and drive for social change in all areas of life. There were no limits to the areas of life that were influenced by the ideas of the Reformation. Martin Luther was angered by the errors of the church and abuses of its doctrinal practices and expressions, and he was moved by a personal crisis of faith to search the Word for something that would rekindle some hope. In Ephesians 2:8–9 he found a text that says we are justified by grace alone, not by works—referring to the love of God that fills the whole earth through the sacrifice of Christ. It is from this love that hope springs. It is this hope born of grace that gives rise to the new things of the Spirit.

These principles of the Reformation give us a paradigm for proceeding with a series of faithful reforms of theological education for our own time. This would involve the work of having theological conversations in each of our church structures and across our church structures. It would mean returning to our structures and looking at our mission and the ways we teach at our theological institutions, so that the mission can be accomplished by our churches. The principles of the Reformation open up for us the theological paradigms for reforming the curricula in light of the present world circumstances.

The times are ripe for reform. As we saw in chapter 1, the Panama Congress proposed that the purpose of Christian education was to "put prayer daily in the mouth of non-Christians. Religious teaching in schools and colleges is aimed at Christians and non-Christians alike. Education is to train in the practices of devotional life creating the importance of habits of private and public prayer, devotional use of the Bible and the practice of the presence of God."[1] The legacy of this conference still shapes Latinx visions of theological education. But what does this vision include, and what does it not include?

The Panama Congress's ideal was of holistic character and personality formation, and the assumption was that this should be done by paying attention to the dimensions of a personal devotional life. But what of the other dimensions of our lives? All real evangelism involves not just devotional life but also *discipleship*. And discipleship shapes the gospel values of the kingdom of God in our midst. Every ideology has an ethic that shapes the principles and practices of morality. For the Christian, values embody theological considerations and deal with what is virtuous, meaningful, and enduring. From these emanate the goals, ideals, and guidelines of the limits of human thought and behavior for everyday life. Real evangelism produces such gospel values.[2]

The gospel values establish the basis for judging all forms of human behavior and the different ideologies that support other forms and systems of living. For example, what does it mean to live in a context where corruption and colonization reign? How can we preach Jesus Christ as Lord of these corrupt authorities? Disciples must pray, for certain. But our gospel values demand more. Discipleship teaches us the way of thinking, or the arguments we use, to understand life according to the will of God. It also teaches us the acceptable practices of Christians based on the Word of God. What arguments of our formation as disciples help us face the challenges of unjust structures? What kind of education would do the most to nurture Christian formation that can resist injustice?

Doing theology is about answering these questions. Theology is an integral part of the church's witness of faith and of how we as church use our understanding of the gospel to address the challenges of her present reality. This connects the doing of theology to the mission of the church. The mission of the church is not a discrete program but an entire lifestyle. Missiologist Orlando Costas says the following of this connection: "The mission of the church gives birth to theology in the measure that it produces a faithful, obedient missionary community for whom the 'search for meaning' (Anselm) becomes a perpetual vocation. There can be no Christian theology without the church."[3] As the church lives incarnationally, walking alongside the people of the community where she is located, she shares in the pain and brokenness of her neighbors. From this suffering will come deeply felt questions about the nature of her faith and mission and its implications for theological education.

Musings and Proposals: New Topics for Dialogue

Latin@ Christians are already asking these questions and listening for answers. In what follows, I present a range of musings and actions on theological education proposed by different Latin@

voices. They show how different groups and thinkers in the church—pastors, laypeople and theologians, practitioners and academics—have drawn on the spirit of *sola fide* and *sola Scriptura* to begin to imagine the new things of the Spirit. I encourage you to stay with each presentation, even if the language used does not feel as familiar to you as your own. I will define terms along the way. Let this be a space in which we listen to one another in our diverse languages as we discern the common yearnings of the Spirit within ourselves as a diverse community. This is a space for both the familiar and the unfamiliar, for discernment and openness, for listening to the healing of the past for the sake of future generations. Expect to hear things you may have denied or rejected before, but please stay the course for the sake of the dialogue and the possibility that the Spirit might just be in these different perspectives.

Lament

Pentecostal theologian Samuel Solivan proposes "orthopathos" as a bridge between the orthodox tradition and the praxis of the church.[4] Orthopathos describes a way to transform human suffering into a resource for liberation. When persons share their suffering narratives as a community of faith, those narratives become testimonies in which God enters the story of suffering or the one telling the testimony. The narrators speak of the presence or absence of God as they share a journey from alienation to wholeness. For this to happen, we need not only to share what is experienced on the surface—the spiritual or psychological pain—but also to inquire further about the deeper roots of the cause of the sufferings (e.g., governmental or institutional policies) and then ask what the community might do to change this. This action uses the narrative of orthopathos for informing and moving toward an action that addresses the suffering. This action is orthopraxis.

This deeper reflection turns the testimony narrative into praxis. Sometimes in this journey, we question the very roots of the theology or the orthodoxy of the faith. This can be a very delicate and even fraught matter, for it leads to the dissection of beliefs that have been held for a lifetime. One must be pastorally sensitive and accountable when bringing persons along such paths. After the shock and loss that result from this dissection, new understanding moves us closer to liberation. The loss entails the fallen idol images of our faith and a journey toward a new understanding of faith. Sharing the experiences and journeys, as well as reflecting critically, can then lead to an action. At a Bible institute, this discussion about action can lead to new ministerial understandings that move from ministerial practice to orthopraxis: reflection *and* action. We have not always stopped to reflect on our ministerial actions. This additional part helps us to be more intentional about doing theology, which in turn can help to lead us to a better-informed theological education.

I witnessed the dynamics of orthopathos firsthand in my time with a community in Puerto Rico. I had the opportunity to teach a community traumatized by Hurricane Maria and a series of earthquakes about the biblical tradition of lament. To make room for lament, we first had to dissect the theology of triumphalism from which the community had been operating. I asked questions that I knew triumphalism did not resolve. I contrasted triumphalism to the psalms of lament and encouraged persons to express themselves in that biblical pattern. The result was a wave of emotions and freedom in the Spirit to question God and to listen to God in new ways that eventually led to a deeper appreciation of God, similar to that of the biblical lament tradition. This community shared the same process with others and unleashed the healing power of the Spirit.

This kind of lamentation broke with what the community had been taught. But it was thoroughly biblical. Indeed, I would argue that it was more faithful to the biblical witness than a triumphalism that ignores deep suffering. The Bible is the central text of study at Latin@ Bible institutes and churches. It is also the text that colonizers have used to interpret to us who we are and what our place is in the world. The Bible is the text that undergirds all the theology and doctrines that define the traditions of the church and, in turn, our worldview. Because these foundational doctrines are based on the Bible, they are considered a truth that cannot be altered. This means that any interpretation that does not fit into the paradigm of determined truth is considered heretical. Can the faithful not question this "truth" in light of the movement of the Holy Spirit in the midst of cultural changes and the crisis of their present historical situation? Can we not question these colonizing interpretations *on the basis of Scripture itself?* What would happen if we reexamined our tradition in light of the Scriptures, just as the church did in the Reformation? Is it possible that through this illumination of the text we could deepen and expand the tradition so that the Latin@ church can gain the understanding that reinforms her mission in the present?

Political Advocacy

What might a bishop do when the congregations under his care are deeply affected by the practices of the Immigration and Customs Enforcement (ICE) agency, when families, and in particular children, are suffering from trauma and depression due to the detention and deportation of their parents? When even his pastors are deported? Can the Latin@ bishop take political action against these rules and measures when the leaders of the ecclesial bodies are made up of the white citizens of the land who believe in rigid obedience to the laws of the land? How can he think theologically when the theology that informs him prohibits him from taking action politically? The rule that prohibits him from taking action comes from another time and place when the North Atlantic missionaries were in our lands of origin. Their theology forbade the bishop from taking political action, for this would have involved disobedience to the rulers of the land. They had a string of prooftexts, isolated snippets of Scripture, to justify their position. But what happens when the bishop reads again the story of Moses confronting Pharaoh and demanding emancipation for the children of Israel? What happens when he starts to become involved in advocacy, even with unbelievers, when, out of his theological reflection and despair, he has come to understand that this is a way to work toward righteousness or justice for the people of the congregations he pastors? How might the bishop draw on fresh readings of Scripture, grounded in the experience of his people and illumined by the Holy Spirit, to revise the theology and in so doing refresh the tradition?

Because the *evangélica* church turns to the Scriptures to refresh the tradition, it is important that we reflect on how we read the Bible. Colonizers presented their own readings as the only possible readings, and it can seem that disagreeing with colonizing readings is disagreeing with the Bible itself. But this is not so, for there is a gap between the colonizers' interpretation of the Bible and the Bible as the living Word of God. Seeing this gap leads us into the process of *hermeneutics*.

Hermeneutics is the task of interpreting, explaining, and appropriating the Word of God in the specific historical situation of the interpreter, bearing in mind the political, social, and economic factors present in it. Ecuadorian evangelical theologian C. René Padilla claims that when we do not include all these factors, we cannot make full meaning.[5] The seeming inflexibility of the interpretation of the Word beyond the "truths" prescribed by the missionaries has created confusion for the Latin@ church in a time of crisis for the community as well as many changes in the present society, including generational changes of perspectives within her own families. Second-generation young adults, and children from subsequent generations, are not able to connect their present lives to the Latin@ church, not only for reasons of language but also because the church's paradigms of "truth" will not respond to the current crisis by considering social justice a part of her mission. To connect with these lives, the church needs a renewed sense of what Padilla termed *misión integral* (holistic mission). A hermeneutics of holistic mission lets us see the ways the biblical text is speaking to us today.

It is out of our present moment that we pose questions to the biblical text. These same questions are the theological questions of our community in this time. Theology must allow for the engagement between the experience of the reader, and the text and its own horizon. God, through the Holy Spirit, meets us in this engagement. The more the reader knows about the present realities, or *vivencias*, and the past realities of the text, the richer the understandings and questions asked.

All readers bring certain theological "preunderstandings" to the work of reading the text. These are ways of making sense that are prior to any particular reading. They both make possible and limit our comprehension of the text. Openness to continuous reading and refinement of these understandings helps us as a community that loves the God encountered in the text. We accept that the worldviews, theologies, and assumptions of these interpretations have framed our interpretation of our historical situation and our understandings of Scripture. In the classroom, we identify these frameworks and recognize how they condition understanding, while also remaining open to the mystery of the illumination that comes to us in each reading through the voices of many in the community. This also leaves room for the sciences of economics, sociology, social psychology, and anthropology to ask questions of Scripture and illuminate it from different angles.

Reason alone is not the epistemological tool for the reading of the Scripture. To gain more than an intellectual comprehension, we need the illumination of the Holy Spirit, who activates the text's meaning in each concrete historical context. This takes place when the interpreter wishes to engage Scripture with the purpose of engaging God about what it means to be faithful in a given situation. This meaning making is a community of faith's appropriation of the biblical text that makes it incarnate in the present moment. It makes possible the Word's breaking into our new situations. This illumination may necessitate the expansion and deepening of the tradition.

This reflection as discernment by the community of faith leads to a doing of theology. We understand that all theology bears the marks of the tensions of its history and the knowledge of its time. We are seeking an epistemological construct for theology and hermeneutics that is not as deeply embedded in Western colonizing ideology.

Revelation is foundational to our conversation about the knowledge of God through the faith. It entails not only the transmission of a body of knowledge but also the self-disclosure of God within history, which has its climax in Jesus of Nazareth. This understanding of revelation implies the combination of a cognitive knowledge of God (doctrines) and a personal relationship of God with humanity in the everyday life, *lo cotidiano*.

For Latinx in the United States, a number of experiences shape the questions we ask when we pray, study the Bible, or talk about our faith to one another. The experiences that have chiefly shaped Latinx theology are those of conquest, colonialism, migration, and biculturalism. The history of Latinx peoples has included the military aggression of North Atlantic nations, which has left entire peoples economically and politically powerless. That history of conquest and colonialism has contributed to a trail of migration. We migrants have been shaped by the experience of being uprooted from our culture and all our personal relationships. This entails economic and social hardship, not least because one cannot always count on benefits and rights being extended by the host country, let alone being able to anticipate what the next day will bring.

The very realities of such a context—urban poverty and violence, ecological disregard, drugs, crime, unemployment, and intolerance for peoples of different cultures and religions—continuously confront us with the limits of our theological traditions. This challenges us to raise questions about our personal experiences in light of Scripture. With practice, such questioning becomes intuitive reflection in one's life. When these reflections are shared communally, we are doing theology. An example of this is to look at a text such as Psalm 37 and ask in our present time of the COVID-19 pandemic: How is it that the majority of persons affected by the virus are living in poorer conditions and with jobs in the service sector that are paid the least?

The process of interrogating one's experience in light of Scripture entails both a discontinuity and a continuity of the tradition. The continuity entails handing on or transmitting the tradition. At the same time, the very nature of the tradition requires that we critique it in order to reactualize it. To reactualize it is to use the tradition not to invoke and repeat the past but to see what it reveals about the present and the future. The tradition then interprets present experience and "the past speaks to the present for the sake of the future,"[6] thus creating a dialectic among the three. The tradition then becomes a living, ongoing tradition that fosters liberation. The tradition is reactualized in order to renew our understanding of our time and our sense of mission in that time. By interrogating our experience in light of Scripture, we are doing what the Reformers did. We are letting a fresh, Spirit-filled reading of Scripture question the structures of a tradition that aligned itself with oppression. We are trying to live *sola Scriptura* lives.

The bishop in the midst of the immigration dilemma is engaging in work like this. He is reading the story of the exodus, the oracles of the prophets, and testimonies to the liberative work of Jesus. Together these readings reveal a God who walks with those who are oppressed and calls people of faith to challenge the powers and principalities that oppress them. His faithful reading of Scripture convinces him that discipleship or practical obedience is best expressed through the work of advocacy along with others (whether they are from the church or not). His reading leads him to enter into this discernment with others asking for the illumination of the Word of God in light of this dilemma, and then with confidence to redefine the mission of the church and, subsequently, its theology. This hermeneutical process is a way of decolonizing the reading of Scripture and the doing of theology. It involves reading Scripture to purify our reading of Scripture: *sola Scriptura*. Inspired by the Reformers, it is a mode of faithful practice.

Behold Nuevas Cosas: Theology, Globalization, and New Generations

New spaces are emerging where millennials and Generation Z are practicing new forms of ministry by way of podcasts, activism, and healing. These younger Christians are moving these ministries to social media and nonprofits as well as describing them in books they write that integrate the knowledge and wisdom from their lives with the ministries they are carrying out while working to sustain themselves. They weave together the different parts of their education from universities, yoga classes, and traditional theological education, all of which have helped them to form a sense of how best to contribute to make the world a place of justice.

As they form new rituals and renew or reprise older ones, they bring meaning to their work in the world with God. Fellowship is formed in online spaces; hashtag dialogues are their reflective spaces. I've noticed that in their nonprofits there are spaces on their boards for elders—those who have brought wisdom and resources upon which the younger folks are now establishing their own work. Wisdom is considered a mystical, inner part of the spiritual tradition that does not contain the doctrinal legalisms or structures that are tainted with what these younger Christians consider the hypocrisy of religion that does damage to persons' souls.

Mission for these younger generations of Christians refers to the many expressions through which one brings social justice, healing, and immediate help to those suffering. Teachers in these settings, such as Agustin Quiles of Mission Talk, bring things new and old out of their coffers from different traditions or from the one they have known. Theological education that gives access to these coffers, that opens up spaces for persons to weave new tapestries and make new colors of threads, is calling. This signifies that we are at the brink of exploring uncharted ground. As we explore such ground, are we ready to give consideration to theological ideas and experiences that seem heretical at first glance? Can we listen to one another's experiences of the Spirit to discern the new places that the Spirit may be taking us? Or are we closing off those places of listening and discernment out of fear of walking beyond the orthodox parameters of our faith as we have received it? Fear too often leads us to judge and label each other even before we have finished understanding each other.

In light of much that is new, and so much that necessitates that we come together as fellow humans, what might glimpses of the new creation look like? Are there things that our forefathers and foremothers in the faith rejected that might contain the thread of truth we need for the tapestry of our faith today as we move into the future?

Whether or not we even feel comfortable considering such questions, Generation Z is already asking them and is unearthing their past and the lesser-known roots of Christianity as sources of their faith. Theological education must delve into the questions and the variety of answers and new paradigms within which these explorations fall. As Christian leaders, we can't stand by without a way to engage their questions within their paradigms and not ours if we are to hold a substantive dialogue of faith. In this dialogue we trust the Spirit to lead us together into all truth, a truth that for now we can see only dimly through a glass (1 Cor. 13:12).

What might "all truth" look like? What will be the "new things"? Theologian Oscar García-Johnson considers the "rhizomatic nature of God's revelation"[7] in order to embrace a transoccidental mestizo hermeneutic that can bring together different mediations of the divine with the purpose of "forming a web of human solidarity until [we] construct . . . the body of Christ."[8] He interprets these philosophical arguments through the lens of Pentecost, where Pentecost is not a private religious event but one that takes place in a public space and is open to persons of all ethnicities, religious beliefs, and walks of life. García-Johnson seeks a way to consider the beliefs of those who were rejected and suppressed by a colonizing Christianity, a way of considering their beliefs that does not oppress the religious beliefs of the different peoples that make up the Americas. He seeks to retrieve the ways in which, had it not been for the prejudices of the church, we would have seen how the different communities already had a witness of God and how they interpreted this God as one who was Creator of heaven and earth and was above all other gods.

To do this, García-Johnson goes to the sources of descriptions of the peoples' beliefs as seen by the theologians of the church at the time. Because we never explored the glimpses of God in the native peoples' religions, we missed the opportunity to see God revealed in ways we had not imagined. But instead of such a discernment process, there was a process of systemic violence. The dialogue never took place. Without a true understanding of the different religions, we nonetheless demonized them, lifting up the seemingly bizarre in them. For García-Johnson, the way to look again at this is to be guided by the Holy Spirit, whom he calls the decolonizing healer.

He posits that "healing is ecological as it is also political and cultural. Therefore, healing is liberation and liberation is healing," so that the "Spirit of God abides, transmits, gives life and healing to subjugated lands and peoples."[9] He mentions the ways in which this Spirit has been present in the indigenous communities of original Americans and gives examples of these. He refers to the Paraclete as the Spirit outside the gate, meaning outside of the gate of Western Christianity. García-Johnson sees discernment as the way in which the Spirit "aims at opening up the possibility of constructive friendship and mutual understanding with non-western religious traditions," which would help us to create spaces for embracing theological diversity.[10] This is extremely important to the new generations who seek to live in more inclusive ways among the diversity that touches them every day, rather than continuing to resort to exclusionary discourses and practices.

In a globalized society, we find ourselves face-to-face with a greater diversity than our world of ideas has ever embraced before. Generation Z will be the most diverse generation in the history of the United States. The Latinx community will form a large part of that generation. This diversity includes different religious expressions—and no religious expression. When almost 25 percent of the youth of our churches are leaving because their generational needs are not met by the church of their parents, when those youth are no longer comfortable with a theological paradigm that excludes their friends' lifestyles and religions, when their understanding of God and love does not resonate with that of their friends, how do we reflect theologically with them? How do we begin with a premise of discovering options to their faith questions and restlessness that may even be different from the positions we had previously held? Our fear that the young people might not land in the places we have called "sound doctrine" has held us back from such a starting point. But here we should cling not to our own doctrine but to God alone—*sola fide!*—trusting the Spirit to guide us together into all truth.

Beyond Clericalism: Theological Education for a Misión Integral

The Latinx population will have a Generation Z that will be the most educated generation we have ever had. Their faith quest will need to include an interdisciplinary dialogue that facilitates an understanding of calling as a professional in arenas of work and society other than the church, as well as a deeper conversation about stewardship that includes ecological aspects of the care of creation and what to do with a level of wealth and opportunities to which their parents never had access. What values will inform the lifestyles they can now afford?

In his edited book *Looking Forward with Hope: Reflections on the Present State of Theological Education*, Benjamin Valentín redefines the mission and purpose of the freestanding Protestant seminary. Valentín takes the reader beyond the traditional understanding of the purpose of theology and the mission of a seminary of training for church professions to "the fostering of other 'professions' and pursuits aimed at the search for transcendence and the building of a more sacred, compassionate, just and peaceful world."[11] Bible institutes that are being intentional about addressing the spiritual needs of young adults are creating new courses that intentionally look at the professions and the doing of social justice. This too is a glimpse of the new things of the Spirit.

This new generation will face globalized realities that are unprecedented and which call for globalized, interdisciplinary conversations even beyond the present parameters of the church and its mission.[12] Faithfulness to a *misión integral* will involve not just openness to preparing students for other vocations but also a willingness to listen more deeply and widely in our traditions. In his book *Brown Church: Five Centuries of Latino/a Social Justice and Identity*, scholar Roberto Chao Romero tells of five hundred years of this legacy, narrating for us the central figures and thought of advocacy and social justice during each season of oppression and across the Americas from the Spanish colonization to the farm workers movement in the United States. He uncovers a rich legacy and discussion of Latinx faith and identity. Reaching into the past to fertilize the future with prophetic boldness is important, for together the different generations can share a new horizon of the mission of the church in a different season. This dialogue is spiritually formational and prepares the generations to pass and to receive the baton. Theological education informed by a vision of *misión integral* will draw upon the full depth and breadth of this dialogue.

Signs of New Things: Bivocational Pastors and Scholars

In these times, some leaders of institutes and denominations are responding to the challenges of ministry by focusing on the spiritual formation of pastors because the inner life of the pastor is important to sustaining discipleship and the mission of the church. They are paying attention to the task of doing theology, listening to and noticing the signs of the times through the ears and eyes of our new generations, and asking theological questions about our rapidly advancing use of technology and social media.

In asking these questions, spiritually attentive listeners are starting to hear new answers. This is especially true around young people's sense of *vocation*. Twenty years ago we used to ask young people what they wanted to become. The answer would identify a particular profession. Today, however, the question is: "What are you passionate about?" The question leaves open the issue of how that passion can be fulfilled. Attending to the vocations of young people today opens us to the significance of Christian leadership in institutions beyond the congregation. Community organizing, for instance, has become a necessary pastoral skill. Organizing might be rooted in a congregation. But it reaches beyond the congregation to the wider community.

As vocations of faithful service multiply, connection and conversation among them become more and more important. Relationships between scholars and church leaders are especially significant. Out of their prophetic vision, networkers are encouraging and facilitating relationships among us that were not possible before, and the bishops of the church are clamoring to hear the voices of their church scholars. On the Mestizo Podcast, Bishop Angel Marcial of the Church of God confirms that church leaders need to hear the scholars and what they have to say about the new generations, theology, and the mission of the church.[13] He calls for such a dialogue and for the theological education of church leaders.

The dialogue between scholars and church leaders is a very important one. We will need to approach each other with appreciation for our gifts, as Bishop Marcial's invitation implies, valuing the experiences we bring and the love for the people we serve in different ways. In the dialogue, we will learn each other's languages, and we will learn how to ask each other questions in the places where previously we might have judged each other and truncated the dialogue. As we persist in our love not only for one another and God but also for the world, including every creature in the creation, we will do the works that Christ has done, and even greater works (John 14:12).

Discerning the need for vocations that serve God in these

times also awakens us to the importance of bivocational work. Colonizers have often looked down on scholars who straddle church and academy, seeing bivocational service as something like a stage that should be outgrown with greater training and financial resources. But we would note the remarkable vitality of bivocational scholars and the communities they serve. These scholars have interwoven their scholarship with the pastorate or activism. They have cross-fertilized one with the other. Being in two different contexts creates hermeneutics of integration as well as a spirituality of the scholar that employs discernment as a process of life. Scholars who walk in different realms simultaneously take a while to negotiate this dual navigation as they make a space of freedom for creating a hybrid vocation where they are able to speak to the church with authority as well as to the academy. Such scholars open up the controls of theologies of white supremacy and colonization embedded in the church without the fear of being ostracized because they have created the trust (*confianza*) necessary with the community of faith with whom they walk and for whom they care daily. The conversations that take place are spaces of grace where the scholar is able to speak with a fully authentic voice and inner authority while facilitating space for the development of the voices of others. Such a space is where scholars say that God is creating "*una capirotada*" or "*un mogollo.*" Both words mean similar things to different cultural groups—a mix of many things. These "mixed" or "blended" vocations are not something to be outgrown. They are sources of strength and insight.[14]

Whether in or beyond congregations, whether singular or blended, vocations today place great demands on people. Young people seem to recognize this, and they are especially interested in developing their spirituality as they go about the work of changing the world as an expression of their passions. Theological education for these times must attend not just to skills but also to the cultivation of deep and durable spirituality.

Theological education for these changing times will also involve new kinds of institutions. Young people are already creating virtual spaces for reflection, peer mentoring, and dialogue. Podcasts or Zoom parties for theological reflection are examples of such spaces. Those who have grown up learning from the Internet and online are more autodidactic. Their interest is in the application of knowledge as an expression of their spirituality and passions, and not in degrees for theological education. This makes theological education less a repository and more a companion on a journey. Competency-based education, with the freedom to create a custom-made curriculum, is one way to gather the energy from this type of learning. Certificates or badges are another way. In devising such plans, schools are just scrambling to catch up with the realities students are already creating.

Spiritual Anticipation

The Gospel of Luke tells of the moving of the Spirit as she prepares new things. The Spirit appears to Zacharias, makes it possible for him and Elizabeth, his wife, to have a child even though they are beyond their childbearing years. This child will prepare the way for the Messiah. The Spirit then comes to Mary to tell her of God's plan to overshadow her, making it possible for her to bear Emmanuel, "God with us." The Spirit leaps in the womb of Elizabeth when the unborn child within her hears Mary's voice. The Spirit is also present in Simeon. When Joseph and Mary bring the child Jesus to be dedicated in the temple, a routine ritual, Simeon discerns that this child is the long-awaited Messiah. The widow Anna also is able to see what the Spirit is doing, and she tells others about the child of hope who has come into their midst.

The new things of the Spirit are usually unexpected—surprises that come to us in ways that transgress our accustomed religious interpretations and traditions. We can respond only if we have learned through our spiritual discipline how to be spiritually discerning in how we interpret and critique the tradition and how to be open to the unforeseen and bewildering happenings, dialogues, and invitations of the Holy Spirit who is outside the gate.

We find ourselves in a time when the forms of "church" are transitioning. But we do not yet know what the new forms will look like because they are still in the making. For now, we have in our midst the "church" we have known for centuries and its diverse structures. We are different generations seeking God in different ways. "The wind blows wherever it pleases. You hear its sound, but you cannot tell where it comes from or where it is going. So it is with everyone born of the Spirit" (John 3:8). The Spirit is blowing in a new way, not only among Latin@ Christians but also among people around the world. Cathedrals are becoming religious artifacts rather than places of worship. They may at times be spaces of beauty that inspire the mystic soul toward God or places for holding religious events, but more rarely are they places inhabited by a steady worshiping community identified with the community that surrounds it.

So it is that the expressions of Christianity among the younger generations become more mobile, virtual, and mystical. Theological education may become more of a journey that responds to the needs of that pilgriming community of discernment and activism than an institutional place with courses representing academic or church traditions to be transmitted. Let us follow the Spirit, who, like the wind, is universal, unpredictable, and outside our control. As the wind of the Spirit blows, it first prepares us for the work to come. It may blow hard enough to empty a room of that which is in the way of the new, thus preparing the way. Sometimes the wind brings something with it and it drops it in our space, filling it with new things. The Spirit comes to fill us with the fullness of God needed in our times to heal trauma and brokenness, to respond to questions that seek a deeper place of understanding of suffering and God, to bring hope to the struggles of reconciliation that persist, to bring thriving to places where life is snuffed out by violence and greed, and to bring beauty to spaces where corruption has defaced the divine.

CHAPTER 5

What wind words are living within you as you teach, dialogue, and engage in missional praxis?

> The God who created the cosmos, stretched out the
> skies,
> laid out the earth and all that grows from it,
> Who breathes life into earth's people,
> makes them alive with his own life:
> "I am God. I have called you to live right and well.
> I have taken responsibility for you, kept you safe.
> I have set you among my people to bind them to me,
> and provided you as a lighthouse to the nations,
> To make a start at bringing people into the open, into
> light:
> opening blind eyes,
> releasing prisoners from dungeons,
> emptying the dark prisons.
> I am God. That's my name.
> I don't franchise my glory,
> don't endorse the no-god idols.
> Take note: The earlier predictions of judgment have
> been fulfilled.
> I'm announcing the new salvation work.
> Before it bursts on the scene,
> I'm telling you all about it."
>
> (Isa. 42:5–9 The Message)

Conclusion

As mentioned throughout this book, theological education in the Latinx context exists in a continuum. Within this continuum we are forming persons to love God with all their hearts and minds and strength. We are supporting persons in the fullness of their Christian growth and practices throughout a lifetime. As persons grow in multidimensional ways—professionally, emotionally, and in taking on different roles in their daily lives and relationships—theological education takes on different forms along this continuum to help them address the desire to be faithful as an expression of love to God, others, and all created beings.

Testimonies in the church give evidence of the fact that people are thinking biblically and theologically about their *vivencias*, or lived experiences. They indeed do hunger and thirst for the knowledge that deepens and informs these reflections, which, in an immigrant community, bring order and healing to the chaos and trauma of uprootedness for the first generation that has immigrated and provide guidance and a sense of identity and groundedness for the second and subsequent generations being formed in the diaspora.

The knowledge of God that produces faithful living is incarnational and includes the integration of theology and practice. Church historian and theologian Justo González takes this a step further and posits that we want to learn to think theologically so that we can "employ that knowledge in such a way as to encourage dialogue with the rest of human knowledge." He argues that theological education is a lifelong process whose "final goal is the contemplation of the face of God in the final reign of peace and justice." It is therefore a process of communal as well as private reflection that leads to "constant growth in obedience and service—that is a process of sanctification that is spiritual as well as moral and intellectual."[1]

I have sought to show how this is taking place in different Latin@ contexts by giving an honest picture and analysis of the places of struggle, confrontation, and humility that make this possible. This is more than an intellectual process, and it therefore entails community, for it is in community that we best come to transformation. It also involves action and reflection taking place in a circular fashion. This is the foundation for the doing of theology as *teología en conjunto* (collaborative theology). Helmut Thielicke states that "true theologians think within the community of God's people, and for that community, and in the name of that community."[2] I would like to suggest that the members of the community itself are the theologians. These are theologians whose motivation is the love of God, neighbor, and creation and who have a knowledge that opens up the imagination of compassion.

Contextual faithfulness that seeks to show a glimpse of the *basileia* is not disembodied. This now invites us as theological educators to reflect with imagination upon these matters. What forms are needed for this type of theological education continuum? Where will you look to create the partnerships for the collaborations required to sustain it? What is the educational ecology that you envision? How will this relational dimension of the work transform our racial and socioeconomic perspectives and practices so that these align with the values of the *basileia* and become our obedient service in the world in all our callings and arenas of life—a mission of ambassadors of reconciliation, the good news needed today?

For Further Thought

Teología en conjunto is well read, of course. But it does not stop with reading. It takes the next step of collective, embodied action. If the questions in this book are stirring you, I would encourage you to find a small group of from two to five persons with whom you wish to have a dialogue about these matters. Listen to your lives and the lives of those around you. Return to Scripture with fresh eyes, seeking a vision. Your talk might be wide-ranging at first. But eventually you should pick an area on which you would like to focus your collaboration. Commit to a set of systematic conversations that allow you to strategize for action. As each action is taken, reflect and evaluate, and then plan the next action. This process of studying, talking, listening, acting, and reflecting is not just planning for theological education. It is a theological education in itself. It is the art of using the *cabos sueltos* of *testimonios*, community, collaboration, and the imagination of compassion among others.

Notes

Introduction

1. Unless otherwise indicated, Scripture quotations come from the New International Version (2011).

2. I will use "Latin@" to refer to church and "Latinx" to refer to the community. There are still arguments about the use of both, but at this point it seems that the churches are using "Latin@" to refer to themselves and other community entities are using "Latinx." I wish to honor both.

3. The congregation had decided that they would call this day Pan-American Day.

4. See website of Association for Hispanic Theological Education (AETH), at https://www.aeth.org/?language=english.

5. "Wabash Webinar: Organizational Change, Collaboration, and Creativity," June 4, 2020, https://www.youtube.com/results?search_query =organizational+change%2C+collaboration+and+creativity.

6. For further information, see Stephen Lewis, Matthew Wesley Williams, and Dori Grinenko Baker, *Another Way: Living and Leading on Purpose* (Saint Louis: Chalice, 2020).

Chapter 1

1. "Una persona que tiene una capacidad de criterio, una formación que le permite saber actuar en las situaciones que se le presentan. . . . También una persona bien educada debe tener un conjunto de criterios éticos y actitudes que le hagan aplicarlos en pro de la justicia y del buen hacer." https://www .google.com/search?client=firefox-b-1-d&q=persona+educada+definicion.

2. José Míguez Bonino, *The Faces of Latin American Protestantism: 1993 Carnahan Lectures*, trans. Eugene L. Stockwell (Grand Rapids: Eerdmans, 1997), 6–7.

3. Rosemarie E. Stewart, *United States in the Caribbean* (Oxford: Heinemann Educational Publishers, 1982), 4.

4. Stewart, *United States in the Caribbean*, 4.

5. The Panama Congress Report (Spanish version), Braga-Monteverde, Report No. 2, 41, cited in Míguez Bonino, *Faces of Latin American Protestantism*, 11.

6. Míguez Bonino, *Faces of Latin American Protestantism*, 12.

7. Pan-Americanism is a movement that seeks to create, encourage, and organize relationships, associations, and cooperation among the states of the Americas through diplomatic, political, economic, and social means. See Alonzo Aguilar, "Pan-Americanism from Monroe to the Present," *Monthly Review Press, New York* (1968).

8. Míguez Bonino, *Faces of Latin American Protestantism*, 15.

9. See John Dewey, *Democracy and Education: An Introduction to the Philosophy of Education* (New York: Macmillan, 1916).

10. Dewey, *Democracy and Education*, chap. 1.

11. Dewey, *Democracy and Education*, chap. 1.

12. See *Christian Work in Latin America* (New York: Missionary Education Movement, 1917), vol. 1.

13. "Education in Relation to the Christianisation of National Life," 1910 Conference Report, vol. 3, chap. 9, pp. 322–23.

14. Míguez Bonino, *Faces of Latin American Protestantism*, 16.

15. 2 Timothy 3:16, Amplified Bible.

16. Míguez Bonino, *Faces of Latin American Protestantism*, 40.

17. Míguez Bonino, *Faces of Latin American Protestantism*, 40. See also Pablo A. Deiros, *Historia del Cristianismo en América Latina* (Buenos Aires: Latin America Theological Fraternity, 1992).

18. Míguez Bonino, *Faces of Latin American Protestantism*, 13.

19. Míguez Bonino, *Faces of Latin American Protestantism*, 41. Prudencio Damboriena, SJ, *El Protestantismo en América Latina: Etapas y Métodos del Protestantismo Latino-Americano*, vol. 1 (Friburgo, Colombia: Oficina Internacional de Investigaciones de FERES, 1962), 32, mentions how the number of foreign missionaries in Latin America jumped from 1,707 in 1916 to 6,361 in 1957.

20. Míguez Bonino, *Faces of Latin American Protestantism*, 44. Also see Deiros, *Historia del Cristianismo en América Latina*, 771–72, 801–8.

21. Dewey, *Democracy and Education*, chap. 1.

22. Dewey, *Democracy and Education*, chap. 1.

23. Dewey, *Democracy and Education*, 309.

24. Dewey, *Democracy and Education*, 406.

25. Dewey, *Democracy and Education*, 444.

26. See David K. Naugle, *Worldview: The History of a Concept* (Grand Rapids: Eerdmans, 2002).

27. "Definición de cosmovisión—Qué es, Significado y Concepto," http://definicion.de/cosmovision/#ixzz4BUZ7vUFu.

28. Roberto Pazmiño, *Cuestiones Fundamentales de la Educación Cristiana* (Miami: Editorial Caribe, 1995), 108.

29. Pazmiño, *Cuestiones Fundamentales*, 109.

30. Paul H. Vieth, *Objectives in Religious Education* (New York: Harper & Brothers, 1930), 70–78.

31. Vieth, *Objectives in Religious Education*, 148.

32. Carlos Raúl Sosa Saliézar, "Aportes misionológicos del protestantismo liberal en América Latina," *Teología y Cultura* 8, no. 4 (December 2007): 49.

33. Saliézar, "Aportes misionológicos," 52. See also Jorge P. Howard, *La Otra Conquista de América* (Buenos Aires and Mexico City: Editorial La Aurora y Casa Unida de Publicaciones, 1951).

34. Howard, *La Otra Conquista de América*, 144–45.

35. Sherron Kay George, "Ecumenical Theological Education in Latin America, 1916–2005," *International Bulletin of Missionary Research* 31, no. 1 (2007): 15.

36. This point will be fleshed out in more detail in chapter 3, on curriculum.

37. Kenneth F. Woods, "Samuel Guy Inman—His Role in the Evolution of Inter-American Cooperation" (Washington, DC: American University, 1962), 28.

38. Woods, "Samuel Guy Inman," 30.

39. Woods, "Samuel Guy Inman," 30.

40. Woods, "Samuel Guy Inman," 33.

41. Woods, "Samuel Guy Inman," 35.

42. Samuel Silva Gotay, *Protestantismo y Política en Puerto Rico: 1898–1930; hacia una historia del protestantismo evangélico en Puerto Rico* (San Juan, Puerto Rico: Editorial de la Universidad de Puerto Rico, 1998), 248–49.

43. *Panama Congress, 1916*, vol. 1, *Christian Work in Latin America, Survey Occupation, Message, and Education* (New York: Missionary Education Movement, 1916), 508.

44. Quote from Dr. Harris, director of the Instituto Politécnico de San German in Puerto Rico. Cited in Silva Gotay, *Protestantismo y Política en Puerto Rico*, 249.

45. Silva Gotay, *Protestantismo y Política en Puerto Rico*, 214.

46. Silva Gotay, *Protestantismo y Política en Puerto Rico*, 214.

47. "This we heard from Rev. Drury in Puerto Rico." Silva Gotay, *Protestantismo y Política en Puerto Rico*, 247.

48. See George, "Ecumenical Theological Education in Latin America," 16–19.

49. Damboriena, *El Protestantismo en América Latina*.

50. Damboriena, *El Protestantismo en América Latina*, 75.

51. Latin@ churches in the United States still deal with this theological influence. A part of theological education that is contextual has included theological reflection and social analysis that help to forge a different theological thinking (and a *pastoral* that emerges from that thinking) capable of addressing socioeconomic and political issues, such as the unjust laws and policies of immigration.

52. Damboriena, *El Protestantismo en América Latina*, 76.

53. Panama Congress Report 2, 281–82, 449, cited in Silva Gotay, *Protestantismo y Política en Puerto Rico*, 76.

54. Damboriena, *El Protestantismo en América Latina*, 77.

55. Yorke Allen Jr., *A Seminary Survey: A Listing and Review of the Activities of the Theological Schools and Seminaries Located in Africa, Asia, and Latin America Which Are Training Men to Serve as Ordained Ministers and Priests in the Protestant, Roman Catholic, and Eastern Churches* (New York: Harper & Brothers, 1960).

56. Today, these same types of programs take place at Bible institutes. They do not meet the standards for accreditation.

57. For full lists of institutes and seminaries with the details of denominations, number of students, and number of professors, see Damboriena, *El Protestantismo en América Latina*.

Chapter 2

1. José Míguez Bonino, *The Faces of Latin American Protestantism: 1993 Carnahan Lectures* (Grand Rapids: Eerdmans, 1997), 131.

2. Míguez Bonino, *Faces of Latin American Protestantism*, 131.

3. See Jon Sobrino, *The True Church and the Poor* (Maryknoll, NY: Orbis,

NOTES TO PAGES 33-37

1984), and Emilio Castro, *Freedom in Mission: An Ecumenical Enquiry* (Geneva: WCC Publications, 1985).

4. Míguez Bonino, *Faces of Latin American Protestantism*, 143.

5. J. Sepulveda, "Pentecostal Theology in the Context of the Struggle for Life," in *Faith Born in the Struggle for Life*, ed. D. Kirkpatrick (Grand Rapids: Eerdmans, 1988), 299.

6. Taken from the "Final Document" of the meeting of the Encuentro de Pentecostales Latinoamericanos in Salvador, Bahia, Brazil, January 6–9, 1988, 154, published in Carmelo Alvarez, ed., *Pentecostalismo y liberacion* (San Jose, Costa Rica: DEI, 1992) and quoted in Míguez Bonino, *Faces of Latin American Protestantism*, 67.

7. Ruth Padilla Deborst, "Integral Mission Formation in Abya Yala (Latin America): A Study of the Centro de Estudios Teologicos Interdisciplinarios (1982–2002) and Radical Evangelicals" (PhD diss., Boston University, 2016), vi–vii. I am indebted to the material in this dissertation and personal conversation with Ruth Padilla Deborst for much of the historical background to *misión integral* and its making in this chapter. The dissertation features many personal conversations that Padilla Deborst was able to have with the original theologians of this time as well as her access to their personal papers.

8. Padilla Deborst, "Integral Mission Formation," 100. Salvadoran theologian Emilio Antonio Nuñez characterized "evangelical theology" in Latin America as theocentric, bibliocentric, Christocentric, and pneumatological. See Emilio Antonio Nuñez, "Towards an Evangelical Latin American Theology," *Evangelical Review of Theology* 7 (1983): 125–30. The term "radical evangelicals" was used to define this theological understanding. Orlando Costas employed the term as a means to differentiate the FTL both from groups that identified fully with theologies of liberation and from those that rejected it outright. For him, radical evangelicals were people who sought to remain faithful to Scripture and, at the same time, incarnated in the Latin American sociopolitical reality. See Antonio Carlos Barro, "Orlando Enrique Costas: Mission Theologian on the Way and at the Crossroads" (PhD diss., Fuller Theological Seminary, 1993), 24. See also Orlando Costas, "Teólogo en la Encrucijada," in *Hacia una Teología Evangélica Latinoamericana*, ed. C. René Padilla (Miami: Editorial Caribe, 1984), 13–35.

9. C. René Padilla, "Introduction: An Ecclesiology for Integral Mission," in *The Local Church, Agent of Transformation: An Ecclesiology for Integral Mission*, ed. Tetsunao Yamamori and C. René Padilla (Buenos Aires: Ediciones Kairos, 2004), 20.

10. Padilla Deborst, "Integral Mission Formation," 107.

11. I prefer to use the term *basileia*, which is the Greek word for "kingdom of God," because it evokes more neutral and open images or visions. The terms "kingdom of God" (in English) and *reino* (in Spanish) evoke a sense of hierarchy and of patriarchy. These are contrary to the justice and liberation that the vision of the *basileia* represents.

12. Padilla Deborst, "Integral Mission Formation," 107.

13. Padilla Deborst, "Integral Mission Formation," 29.

14. L. L. Belleville, "A Ministry of Reconciliation," http://www.biblegate .com/resources/commentaries/IVP-NT/2Cor/ministry-reconciliation.htm/.

15. See Loida I. Martell-Otero, Zaida Maldonado Perez, and Elizabeth Conde-Frazier, *Latina Evangelicas: A Theological Survey from the Margins* (Eugene, OR: Cascade, 2013), 92.

16. For this brief historical summary of this doctrine, I am indebted to Eastwood Cyril, *The Royal Priesthood of the Faithful: An Investigation of the Doctrine from Biblical Times to the Reformation* (Minneapolis: Augsburg, 1963). From this point on in this chapter, "church" will refer to the Latin@ and Latin American church context.

17. Cyprian, *Letters* 66.8.3.

18. See Martin Lutero, *La Libertad Cristiana* (Buenos Aires: La Aurora, 1983). In English: *On Christian Liberty* (Minneapolis: Augsburg Fortress, 2003).

19. Leonardo Boff, *Ecclesiogenesis: The Base Communities Reinvent the Church* (Maryknoll, NY: Orbis, 1986), 28.

Chapter 3

1. *Concilios* are groupings of congregations that are under one rule. They are perhaps smaller types of denominations that work with different degrees of autonomy, depending on the council.

2. Orlando E. Costas, "Contextualization and Incarnation," *Journal of Theology for Southern Africa* 29 (1979): 23.

3. Costas, "Contextualization and Incarnation," 24.

4. The WCC conference in Bangkok established the right of churches from non-Western countries to have theological freedom from the West to develop their own structure, liturgy, and doctrine, in so doing ending Western theological dominance of mission and theology. Such a construction welcomed the political, social, and economic dimensions of theology and led to a proliferation of contextual theologies and missional expressions.

Contextual theology was included in the field of systematic theology. See also J. L. Mays, "Justice Perspectives from a Prophetic Tradition," *Biblical Interpretation* 37, no. 1 (1972): 5–17.

5. Costas, "Contextualization and Incarnation," 24.

6. Costas, "Contextualization and Incarnation," 30.

7. Costas, "Contextualization and Incarnation," 30.

8. Robert W. Pazmino, "Designing the Urban Theological Curriculum," in *The Urban Theological Education Curriculum: Occasional Papers*, ed. Eldin Villafañe and Bruce Jackson (Boston: CUTTEP, Gordon Conwell Theological Seminary Center for Urban Ministerial Education, 1995), 15.

9. Another explanation of these is offered in Elizabeth Conde-Frazier et al., *A Many Colored Kingdom: Multicultural Dynamics for Spiritual Formation* (Grand Rapids: Baker Academic), 2004.

10. Insights from Doris Garcia, Latina Theological Group discussion, January 12, 2019.

11. Wati A. Longchar, "Globalization: A Challenge for Theological Education, a Third World Perspective," *Ministerial Formation*, July 2001, 8–9.

12. Longchar, "Globalization," 10.

13. Anaida Pascual Moran, "Theo-Feminist Pedagogy: An Emerging Theological Pedagogy with a Liberating and Transforming Vocation," *Ministerial Formation*, July 2001, 41.

14. Nyambura Njoroge, Francoise Faure, and Magali Roussel, "Letter from Staff," *Ministerial Formation*, January 2003.

15. See "En los caminos pedagógicos de la palabra-acción. Aportes para la construcción de una memoria de la hermenéutica bíblica en Colombia, desde la experiencia del equipo de teología popular de Dimensión Educativa, en la década de 1984 a 1994," in *Iglesia de los pobres. Utopía que espera la primavera* (Bogotá: CODICE, 2013), 199–220.

16. Today there is an organization that trains chaplains. They are persons who will encourage and visit others. In some places they work as chaplains to the police or first responders.

17. Alexia Salvatierra, phone conversation, December 2018.

18. A fishbowl experience is where a few persons role-play or have a dialogue while the audience listens.

19. Salvatierra, phone conversation, December 2018.

20. This conversation took place in October 2017 as a part of the Theological Education between the Times project when the team visited Esperanza College in Philadelphia and listened to a panel of participants speak about their experiences and understandings of theological education.

21. Bloom's taxonomy provides a systematic way of describing how a

learner's thinking and performance grow in complexity when mastering academic tasks. See https://www.google.com/search?client=firefox-b-1-d &q=bloom%27s+taxonomy+questions.

22. Etienne Wenger, *Communities of Practice: Learning, Meaning, and Identity*, Learning in Doing (Cambridge: Cambridge University Press, 1998), 43.

23. Insights adapted from Patricia Bonilla, "Communities of Practice within the Context of Hispanic/Latinx Ministry" (unpublished paper, April 2020).

24. Mark K. Smith, "Paulo Freire: Dialogue, Praxis and Education," infed .org, last updated April 4, 2013, http://infed.org/mobi/paulo-freire-dialogue -praxis-and-education/.

Chapter 4

1. The seminary model that is connected to the ecclesial bodies is only one model of the structure that houses theological education. There are also divinity schools housed in universities. My colleagues Mark Young and Dan Aleshire speak more fully about these models in their books in this series. Religious studies departments at colleges and universities are another model. These of course have a different goal and are not connected to the church but to philosophical/anthropological and sociological visions of how religion works in society.

2. For further discussion, see Edwin Aponte, "Friedrich Schleiermacher," in *Beyond the Pale: Reading Theology from the Margins*, ed. Miguel A. De La Torre and Stacey M. Floyd-Thomas (Louisville: Westminster John Knox, 2011).

3. See Charles M. Wood, *Vision and Discernment: An Orientation in Theological Study* (Atlanta: Scholars Press, 1985), 4.

4. Aponte, "Friedrich Schleiermacher," 109.

5. Aponte, "Friedrich Schleiermacher," 8.

6. See Edwin I. Hernandez, Kenneth G. Davis, and Catherine Wilson, "The Theological Education of U.S. Hispanics," *Theological Education* 38, no. 2 (2002): 71–85. Also see Edwin I. Hernandez and Kenneth G. Davis, *Reconstructing the Sacred Towers: Challenge and Promise of Latino/a Theological Education* (Scranton, PA: University of Scranton Press, 2003).

7. Aponte, "Friedrich Schleiermacher," 111.

8. Gary Riebe-Estrella, "Latinos and Theological Education," *Journal of Hispanic Latino Theology* 4, no. 3 (February 1997): 10–11.

9. Elizabeth Conde-Frazier, "Higher Education and Theological Education: Considerations for the Latin@ Evangelical Church Today," in *The His-*

panic Evangelical Church in the United States: History, Ministry and Challenge, ed. Samuel Pagán (Elk Grove, CA: National Hispanic Leadership Conference, 2016), 90–123.

10. Allan Collins and Richard Halverson, "Rethinking Education in the Age of Technology: The Digital Revolution and the Schools" (January 2009), 7, https://www.researchgate.net/publication/264869053_Rethink ing_education_in_the_age_of_technology_the_digital_revolution_and _the_schools. For further reading, see Allan Collins and Richard Halverson, *Rethinking Education in the Age of Technology: The Digital Revolution and the Schools* (New York: Teachers College Press, 2009).

11. See Hernandez, Davis, and Wilson, "The Theological Education of U.S. Hispanics," 71–85.

12. See Sara Mar Murrieta, "The Role of Church Affiliated Hispanic Organizations in Meeting Some Significant Needs of Hispanic Americans in the United States" (PhD diss., United States International University, 1977).

13. Several studies over the last three decades have shown the contributions of Latin@ churches to their communities. See Elba R. Caraballo Ireland, "The Role of the Pentecostal Church as a Service Provider in the Puerto Rican Community, Boston Massachusetts: A Case Study" (PhD diss., Brandeis University, 1990); Eldin Villafañe, *The Liberating Spirit: Toward an Hispanic American Pentecostal Social Ethic* (Grand Rapids: Eerdmans, 1993); Edwin Aponte, "Latino Protestant Identity and Empowerment: Hispanic Religion, Community, Rhetoric, and Action in a Philadelphia Case Study" (PhD diss., Temple University, 1998).

14. See Michael E. Porter and Mark R. Kramer, "The Big Idea: Creating Shared Value," *Harvard Business Review*, January–February 2011, https:// philoma.org/wp-content/uploads/docs/2013_2014_Valeur_actionnariale _a_partagee/Porter__Kramer_-_The_Big_Idea_Creating_Shared_Value _HBR.pdf.

15. Porter and Kramer, "The Big Idea," 9.

16. Porter and Kramer, "The Big Idea," 9.

17. See Charles R. Foster, "Diversity in Theological Education," *Theological Education* 38, no. 2 (2002): 15–37.

18. Foster, "Diversity in Theological Education," 19.

19. Foster, "Diversity in Theological Education," 19. See also Maxine Greene, *Friedrich Schleiermacher* (New York: Teachers College Press, 1978).

20. Foster, "Diversity in Theological Education," 20.

21. Foster, "Diversity in Theological Education," 20.

22. The concept of communities of practice was first proposed by cognitive anthropologist Jean Lave and educational theorist Etienne Wenger in

1991. See their book *Situated Learning, Legitimate Peripheral Participation* (Cambridge: Cambridge University Press, 1991).

23. See the ATS's annual data tables at https://www.ats.edu/uploads /resources/institutional-data/annual-data-tables/2017-2018-annual-data -tables.pdf.

24. See the AETH website, www.aeth.org.

25. See "What Is a Community of Practice?" Wenger-Traynor.com, December 28, 2011, https://wenger-trayner.com/resources/what-is-a -community-of-practice/.

26. "What Is a Community of Practice?"

27. See, for example, E. Wenger, *Communities of Practice: Learning, Meaning and Identity* (Cambridge: Cambridge University Press, 1998).

28. See the Apostolic Assembly website, http://asambleaapostolica.org /english/.

29. *Hispanics: Demographic and Consumer Spending Trends*, Packaged Facts, June 23, 2016, https://www.packagedfacts.com/Hispanics-Demographic -Consumer-10124772/.

30. AETH Handbook of Certification, 4. (This is an internal AETH document for institutions that wish to be certified.)

Chapter 5

1. Education in Relation to the Christianisation of National Life, 1910 Conference Report, vol. 3, chap. 9, pp. 322–23.

2. Education in Relation, 109.

3. Orlando E. Costas, "Educación Teológica y Misión," in *Nuevas Alternativas de Educación Teológica*, ed. C. René Padilla (Buenos Aires: Nueva Creación; Grand Rapids: Eerdmans, 1986), 10. The English in the text is my translation of "La misión da nacimiento a la teología a la medida en que produce una comunidad misionera fiel y obediente para quien la 'búsqueda por el entendimiento' (Anselmo) se convierte en una vocación perenne. No hay iglesia auténtica sin misión así como tampoco puede haber una verdadera teología cristiana sin iglesia."

4. See Samuel Solivan, *Orthopathos: Pathos and Liberation; Toward an Hispanic Pentecostal Theology* (Sheffield: Sheffield Academic Press, 1998).

5. See C. René Padilla, "Hermeneutics and Culture: A Theological Perspective," in *Down to Earth: Studies in Christianity and Culture; The Papers*

of the Lausanne Consultation on Gospel and Culture, ed. John R. W. Stott and Robert Cootie (Grand Rapids: Eerdmans, 1980), 83–107.

6. Mary C. Boys, *Educating in Faith: Maps and Visions* (Kansas City, MO: Sheed & Ward, 1989), 20.

7. "Rhizome" is a biological term that postmodern philosophers Gilles Deleuze and Félix Guattari have applied to describe a theory about multiple points of origin. A rhizome has no beginning or end and can grow from anywhere and everywhere. It is like a mold or fungus that can reproduce from any cell. In the philosophical theory of the authors, the term is used to suggest the place where there is no central point or origin and nothing controls or shapes a particular idea or belief system. Rhizomes simply grow. Even when you take any part of a rhizome out, it isn't damaged. Philosophically this does away with the notion of hierarchies of ideas, beliefs, and interpretations. See Gilles Deleuze and Félix Guattari, *A Thousand Plateaus: Capitalism and Schizophrenia*, trans. Brian Massumi (Minneapolis: University of Minnesota Press, 1987).

8. Oscar García-Johnson, *Spirit outside the Gate: Decolonial Pneumatologies of the American Global South* (Downers Grove, IL: InterVarsity, 2019), 196–97.

9. García-Johnson, *Spirit outside the Gate*, 207.

10. García-Johnson, *Spirit outside the Gate*, 201.

11. Benjamin Valentín, "Embracing a Greater, Higher Calling: Redefining the Mission and Purpose of the Free Standing Protestant Seminary," in *Looking Forward with Hope: Reflections on the Present State of Theological Education*, ed. Benjamin Valentín (Eugene, OR: Cascade, 2019), 46.

12. Even as I write, I am sheltering in place because of the COVID-19 pandemic.

13. See https://www.worldoutspoken.com/podcasts/the-mestizo-podcast/introducing-the-mestizo-podcast. Retrieved December 8, 2020.

14. These insights come from the conversations of community of practice number 5 of ReDET.

Conclusion

1. Justo L. González, *The History of Theological Education* (Nashville: Abingdon, 2015), 121, 128.

2. Helmut Thielicke, *A Little Exercise for Young Theologians* (Grand Rapids: Eerdmans, 1962), 81.